HEALING THE WESTERN SOUL

A Spiritual Homecoming for Today's Seeker

PRAISE FOR *HEALING THE WESTERN SOUL*

"Judith Miller is uniquely placed to advance our grasp of the issues raised in this book…. She has a wealth of personal experience through which she has developed a refined sense of what spirituality means for the 'Western soul;' and she is able to draw on the experiences of those whom she has sensitively guided through psychological and spiritual growth…."

—*Brian L. Lancaster, Ph.D., Emeritus Professor of Transpersonal Psychology, Liverpool John Moores University, UK; Academic Dean for Transpersonal Psychology at the Professional Foundation, UK*

"She has simply looked into the faces of many people who have had Western grounded spiritual experiences and who have had them rejected by both peers and helpers. When those same people had the same experiences subsequently affirmed and explored, they were healed and liberated. Her conclusions are grounded in massive amount of clinical experience.

This is the daring counter-cultural revelation that many of our 'helpers' neglect and even disdain the Judeo-Christian mystical experiences of those who come to them, in spite of the fact that many of our authentic mystical experiences in the West are expressed in those very images and language. I found myself wanting to send a copy of this book to every postmodern person I know with a note saying 'Hey, how about this!'"

—*Paul R. Smith, author of* Integral Christianity: The Spirit's Call to Evolve

"Sage wisdom to share about the spiritual journey and how we can often find in our own backyards what we have set out to discover by pursuing dusty trails leading to exotic places that don't speak to us nearly as clearly."

—*David Lukoff Ph.D., Professor of Psychology at Sofia University in Palo Alto, CA, Co-president of Association of Transpersonal Psychology*

"Miller's argument that Western traditions have moved away from their spiritual beginnings rings true in today's civilized and scientific-based, society…. It's time to explore the more spiritual side of our belief, and Healing the Western Soul is a great place to start."

—*Rev. Kymberley Clemons-Jones, Pastor of Valley Stream Presbyterian Church and author of* Cured But Not Healed

"Dr. Miller takes us on a fascinating spiritual and intellectual journey as a compassionate guide, a brilliant cartographer, and a kind bridge builder between many valleys and hills of psychology and spirituality.... The 'must read' for all people, from the East and West, who want to heal wounds from traditional religions and to find their spiritual home in relation to deep insights from psychology. A great achievement!"

—*Chung Hyun Kyung Ph.D., Professor of Interfaith Engagement, Union Theological Seminary, New York City*

"At a time of global cultural fusion, Judith Miller calls us back to attend to the spiritual forms that we took on consciously and unconsciously in the early years of our development. She insists that our healing has to take place in the tradition we were first at home in, not in traditions and languages that remain exotic to us and consequently lose their power to articulate precisely and to evoke experience with profundity—just as poetry does—in translation."

—*Dr. Melvyn Hill, psychologist and psychoanalyst in private practice on the Upper West Side of Manhattan. As a graduate student at the University of Chicago, he studied with the distinguished historian of religions, Mircea Eliade.*

"In our common work, which is experiential and scientific, she dares more than other psychotherapists and spiritual leaders to help people to heal their deepest wounds and find their authentic spiritual grounding. I appreciate Judith's scientific competence and reliability. And she has a bigger knowledge which is beyond the brain, unspeakable, comes directly from the heart."

—*Ingo Jahrsetz, Dr. Phil., Wittnau, Germany, President of European Transpersonal Association 2009-2013; Founder and Director of Institute of Consciousness Exploration and Psychotherapy; Honorary Chairman of the Spiritual Emergence Network, e.V. (SEN) Germany; Holotropic Breathwork practitioner and trainer*

"...a milestone and a 'must have' for every spiritual seeker and professional working in the field of Psychology, and Psychotherapy who aims to integrate the spiritual dimension in a profound and trustworthy way."

—*Stefan Dressler, M.D., is a psychiatrist and psychotherapist in Freiburg, Germany, who combines psychodynamic psychotherapy with holotropic breathwork.™ He has a special interest in integrating the transpersonal and spiritual level into the work with clients suffering psychotic episodes.*

"The reader will find the clarity of a top-class teacher along with the large vision of the mystic and the sound reasoning of the scholar. Authentic life experience dilemmas, research, and breakthroughs are presented in a very positive, loving and constructive way."

—Vitor Rodrigues, Ph.D., Psychotherapist, past President of the European Transpersonal Association and author of books on Social Criticism, Science-Fiction, Self-Help Manuals, Psychic Defense, and Regression Therapy

"Dr. Miller offers the wisdom and the means for reclaiming our Western spiritual heritage. She also points to the universality of true mystical experiences and insights that, when properly understood, unite East and West."

—Lawrence Edwards, Ph.D., Founder and Director of Anam Cara, President of the Kundalini Research Network, the integrative care clinical manager at Cincinnati Children's Hospital, on the faculty of New York Medical College, and author of The Soul's Journey: Guidance From The Divine Within

"*Healing the Western Soul* is a pioneering breakthrough for personal and cultural healing in our unprecedented global age. Dr. Miller brings to integral focus her remarkable spiritual intelligence, wealth of psychotherapeutic experience and unique skills in assisting many who face spiritual emergencies to a creative frontier. Her central teaching is that we need to go deeper into our home culture, religion, or tradition to tap our spiritual roots, for without claiming the past, it is impossible to move forward. This vital insight is supported by the consensus of our collective endowment of global wisdom and spiritual enlightenment when seen in a dilated global light. For when we dilate our hearts and minds and gain access to the Source of our great spiritual and awakening teachers—Moses, Jesus, Mohammed, Buddha, Krishna, Socrates, Lao Tzu, to name a few—there is a striking consensus that there is an Infinite Force, Infinite Presence, by whatever Name, that sources all our great religious, philosophical, and spiritual traditions."

—Ashok Gangadean, Ph.D., Margaret Gest Professor of Global Philosophy, Haverford College, USA and author of Meditations of Global First Philosophy; Quest for the Missing Grammar of Logos *and* Awakening of the Global Mind: A New Philosophy for Healing Ourselves and Our World *www.awakeningmind.org*

"It is bewildering that, while religion and spirituality seem to be playing such a central role in many people's lives, so little has been done to incorporate this dimension of the human psyche into mainstream psychology. Dr. Judith Miller's book is making a significant contribution in bridging that gap.

—Zana Marovic Ph.D., clinical psychologist, transpersonal psychotherapist, trainer, and Yoga teacher in private practice in Johannesburg, South Africa.

"...a 'must read' not only for clinicians, spiritual counselors, and educators in the field, but for anyone yearning for that spiritual connection that is essential in the course of the evolution of consciousness on a personal and collective basis. Most importantly, it validates the critical need for Westerners to return to their Judeo-Christian roots with a new and informed spiritual perspective."

—John Z. Amoroso, Ph.D., transpersonal psychotherapist and educator, he has developed a unique therapeutic technique called Integrated Imagery, and he is the author of Awakening Past Lives: A Step by Step Guide to Self-Exploration.

"Miller offers a path to help Westerners return to the mystical roots familiar and known to them 'natively' from childhood. At some point, all of us need to return to plumb the depths of our childhood moorings in the Sacred no matter how far reaching and extraordinary our learnings from the other great spiritual traditions worldwide. I agree."

—Rosemarie Anderson, Ph.D., Professor Emerita, Sofia University; Founder and Consultant, "Transpersonal Consultancy"

"Judith Miller shows us a positive side of how to bring people around the world closer together. Her important message is 'To thine own self be true.' Only by first acknowledging and reconnecting with our own Western sacred ground will we be able to authentically become One with people worldwide from different traditions, worldviews, and cultures. Miller's book is indeed a homecoming, a healing, a gift for spiritual seekers. Excellent read!"

—Charles L. Whitfield, MD, author of Not Crazy: You May Not Be Mentally Ill

—Barbara H. Whitfield, author of The Natural Soul: Unity With the Spiritual Energy That Connects Us

"Dr. Judith Miller clearly has a wealth of knowledge and a rich fund of experience with which to guide us towards a spiritual homecoming. Hers is a fierce but loving challenge to face our western divergence from our Judeo-Christian roots. It is a call to look in the mirror: to search honestly and truthfully deep down inside ourselves for what has been lost and to re-connect with this tacit origin within us. An epiphany!"

—Regina U. Hess, Ph.D, is a German clinical psychologist, transpersonal psychotherapist, researcher, and faculty at international transpersonal educational institutes

"Dr. Judith Miller has explored in depth the very root of our Judeo-Christian heritage and modern spiritual crisis. She expresses brilliantly the Zeitgeist of our time: to come fully home to who we are. The book is an excellent guide to this journey."

—Vladimir Maykov, Ph.D., Chair of Transpersonal Psychology, Moscow Institute of Psychoanalysis, and Senior Research Associate, Russian Academy of Sciences

"A great book, a challenging call. If you happen to consider yourself a spiritual softy, don't touch it. Miller makes it very clear that finding your own spiritual way by acknowledging and opening to your Western mystical roots is a very urgent matter these days. Engaging yourself with the book will leave you, in the end, with the deep and reassuring perspective that, beyond any doubt, you will be guided and carried through the jungle. All you have to do is wholeheartedly get on your way."

—Rainer Pervoltz, co-founder of the Chiron Centre in London and the International Institute for Consciousness Exploration and Psychotherapy in Freiburg, transpersonal psychotherapist and trainer, and author: Uber die Kostlichkeit der Distanz, *2009*

"It made me slap my forehead and say 'YES, OF COURSE!' …Judith Miller has some fabulous client anecdotes running through."

—Jane Slade, professional editor, raised in the temple of logic

"Loved it!! …it is absolutely crucial to the West to get this message and for psychology and religion to stop getting in the way of actual soul experience…."

—Gregg Curry, Raised Methodist, retired Minister

HEALING THE WESTERN SOUL

A Spiritual Homecoming for Today's Seeker

by

Judith S. Miller, Ph.D.

Paragon House

First Edition 2015

Published in the United States by
Paragon House
3600 Labore Road
St. Paul, Minnesota

www.ParagonHouse.com

Copyright © 2015 by Paragon House

Library of Congress Cataloging-in-Publication Data

Miller, Judith S.
    Healing the western soul : a spiritual homecoming for today's seeker / by Judith S. Miller, Ph.D.
        pages cm
    Includes bibliographical references.
    ISBN 978-1-55778-917-4 (pbk. : alk. paper) 1. Mind and body. 2. Civilization, Western. I. Title.
    BF151.M55 2015
    204--dc23
                                2014039335

Manufactured in the United States of America

10 9 8 7 6 5 4 3 2 1

    The paper used in this publication meets the minimum requirements of American National Standard for Information Sciences—Permanence of Paper for Printed Library Materials, ANSIZ39.48-1984.

CONTENTS

Praise for *Healing the Western Soul*   *ii*

Acknowledgments   *xiii*

Introduction: Why the Western Soul Needs Healing   *xv*

    Contacting the Soul   xvi

    Our Spiritual Contradiction   xviii

    The Hunger for Spiritual Guidance   xx

    Lost Moorings   xxiii

Part One

OUR WESTERN SPIRITUAL ANGST

Chapter 1

TWO WAYS OF KNOWING   3

    Why Do-It-Yourself Spirituality Doesn't Work   5

    Craig's Experience Was About Healing   7

    The Other Voice Within   9

    Why Spiritual Experiences Cannot be Ignored   11

    Providing "Treatment" versus Supporting a Process 13

Chapter 2

A CRACK BETWEEN THE WORLDS   17

    "Epiphenomena"   21

    Discovering Why Psychology Needs Spirituality   24

    Working Therapeutically With Different
      States of Consciousness   26

    Mysticism is the Wellspring   28

    The Mystical Experience of Eckhart Tolle   29

    Mark's Premature State of Union   32

    The Spiritual Crisis   35

    Our Culture's "Lazy Assumption"   39

CHAPTER 3
WORLDVIEWS AND SUPPORT SYSTEMS   41
    Our Three Dominant Worldviews   44
    Our Support Systems Based on Our Worldviews   45
    Worldviews on Demand   47
    Religion, Our First Support System   48
    Our Second Support System: Psychology and Its
       Multiple Theories and Worldviews   51
    Why Psychology Avoids Spirituality   54
    Janine and the Incurable Brain   56
    The Diagnostic Category "Religious or
       Spiritual Problem"   60
    The New Age Movement and the
       Spiritual-But-Not-Religious   62

PART TWO

OUR WESTERN SPIRITUAL ROOTS

CHAPTER 4
GOD EXPERIENCE   69
    God, an Experience of Divine Love   71
    The Three Faces of God   75
    Our Challenge and Blessing   86

CHAPTER 5
OUR MYSTICAL GROUND   89
    Our Western Spiritual DNA   90
    The Transformative Power of Jesus   91
    Rejecting the Sacred Marriage   92
    The Shame of a Religious Past   96
    The Dominance of Eastern Religions in Psychology   98
    Why I Encourage Western Seekers to "Come Home"   98
    Bob's Impossible Search   100
    Our Spiritual Identity   101
    Why the Western Path is Active   102

The One God   104
The Ever Important Question   106
The Kabbalah and the Duality of Good and Evil   107
Madly in Love with the Same God   108

CHAPTER 6
LIGHT AND DARKNESS   111
Sybille   112
The Reality of Evil   115
Western Dualism   116
What if Inner Darkness Prevails?   117
The Power of Intention   118
About Choice, Commitment and
    Partnership with God   119
When People Cannot Accept Their Inner Light   121
What Exactly are The Voices?   124
The Problem of Living Without Commitment   126
A Case in Point—Mental Illness or Mental Neglect?   127
What if the Darkness Seems too Strong?   129
Creativity Through a Struggle with Darkness   131

PART THREE

OUR WESTERN SPIRITUAL PATH

CHAPTER 7
STAGE ONE: SPIRITUAL AWAKENING   139
The self versus the Self   141
The Stages of Life and the Spiritual Journey   142
The Three Stages of the Western Spiritual Path   143
A Glimpse of the Transcendent—
    The First Characteristic   146
Dreams as a Glimpse of the "Really Real"   147
A Multidimensional Reality   149
Asking Big Questions—The Second Characteristic   150
Three Tattooed Pilgrims   151

Challenges in Spiritual Awakening   154
Resolving the Challenges in Awakening   159
Kinds of Psycho-Spiritual Work: Two Examples   160

CHAPTER 7
STAGE TWO: ILLUMINATION   167
Characteristics of Spiritual Illumination   169
Jewish and Christian Perspectives about Illumination   173
Challenges of Spiritual Illumination   174
A Modern Seeker's Thoughts about
    the Western Spiritual Path   187

CHAPTER 9
STAGE THREE: UNION   189
Union: the final stage   189
Become *Ayin* to Live in God   191
Psychology's Problem with Union   193
Different Ways to Experience Union   196
The Unique Challenge of Intimate and Personal Union
    with Jesus   200
Christ Consciousness and the Power of Love,
    Compassion, and Forgiveness   202

CHAPTER 10
A NEW PSYCHO-SPIRITUAL WORLDVIEW   205
A New Psycho-Spiritual Worldview   209
Some Final Thoughts about Mental Illness
    in the West   210

End Notes   215

Index   225

ACKNOWLEDGMENTS

Healing the Western Soul is dedicated to my husband and best friend Martin Miller. Your unconditional love, trust, and support have helped tremendously in bringing this book to fruition.

Special thanks to Rondi Lightmark—more than an editor, more than a collaborator, and more than a spiritual friend. Much appreciation for your commitment to the book, to the world of spirit, and to my work.

I am grateful to Ingo Jahrsetz—my dear friend and colleague. Our work together in Germany and around the world has greatly enriched me spiritually, personally, and professionally. And it is this work that has strongly influenced the contents of this book.

I feel privileged to have reconnected with Elinor Donahue after many years of having lost touch. Your consultation came at just the right time.

Thanks also to Gordon Anderson and Rosemary Yokoi from Paragon House for your support of the book and, most importantly, its message.

Finally, I feel great respect and love for each of my clients and students who have opened their hearts and souls to me over the years. Many thanks to those whose stories are told in this book and to those whose stories are not told. Please know that *Healing the Western Soul* could not have been written without each of you. Your courage and commitment to the spiritual path—makes our challenging world a better place.

INTRODUCTION: WHY THE WESTERN SOUL NEEDS HEALING

When soul is neglected, it doesn't just go away.

—Thomas Moore, *Care of the Soul,* 1994

I have been a psychologist for nearly 30 years. I've counseled men in a maximum-security prison, and have worked extensively with individuals with a diagnosis of mental illness. Several times a year I travel to Germany to work with descendants of Nazis, many of whom struggle with shame and guilt over the deeds of their country's past. For most of my career, I have been a psychology professor and, since 2000, I have taught future counselors and psychotherapists in the Graduate School of Human Development at Columbia University.

Although my training was anchored in applied clinical and counseling psychology, human development has become my academic home. The reason is that "development" is about growth and realizing potential, which I believe should be psychology's primary concern.

My work allows me to move successfully in the mainstream, yet for much of my adult life I have had a foot in two different worlds: not only in psychology and academia, but also in the arena of spiritual development. This latter focus, initially inspired by dreams and visions experienced since childhood, has set me on the path I follow today. I guide and support people who are on journeys of spiritual development.

I believe the soul is that part of our nature that blends the individual self with divine energy. When we open to our soul's wisdom, we live life fully, feel peace and satisfaction, and help make the world a better place. Today, however, I believe that the souls of many people in the Western world are in need of healing. People have lost access to the wisdom that lives in their core.

My first book, *Direct Connection: Transformation of Consciousness* (2000), is a chronicle of my struggles as a young psychologist trying to make peace with my scientifically-oriented profession, when I knew my experiences of a spiritual reality did not fit. Years later, I am more aware than ever of the existing confusion in the differing worldviews in Western culture. This is having serious repercussions for the emotional wellbeing and stability of millions of people.

Contacting the Soul

I consider my work as "psycho-spiritual" in that spirituality without psychological self-exploration is incomplete. And psychology without spirituality is not very effective. In my work with clients, I combine psychological guidance with a method developed in the 1980s by Czech psychiatrist Stanislav Grof, that he named "Holotropic Breathwork." Some of the stories in this book describe my work with this powerful meditative modality, which helps people contact the soul that is always present if one searches deeply within. This conduit to Spirit needs to be accessed, for spiritual and personal development to take place. Breathwork, as a method, is simple yet profound. It incorporates components for healing that are universal, having been documented cross-culturally throughout history. During a session—which lasts several hours—people lie down in a group, on mats, in a dimly lit room. With eyes closed, they breathe a little more deeply and rapidly than normal, while powerful music is played in the background. As a person relaxes, the part of the mind that worries, plans, analyzes, and fantasizes slowly gets drawn into the music, becomes the music, and then comes to stillness. Consciousness expands. The busyness of life recedes, and other aspects of the self, such as feelings, sensations, dreamlike images, visions and symbols rise out of the soul. Many of the symbols and resonate with universal truths. At the same time, it is important to realize that whatever particular symbols come up for people are not random. Rather, they provide information as to what area(s) of life the person needs to develop or change. The visions often come from the great religions and mystical traditions that have been part of humanity's history. A different way of self-knowing is the harvest of the time spent. When the session is over, people share and discuss the implications that their experiences might have on their daily lives. Here, psychology plays a part in putting things into perspective.

I have been facilitating this work for more than 20 years with thousands of people in America and Europe. What I witness over and over is that most participants whose spiritual roots are connected to the Judeo-Christian tradition will at some point access a level of consciousness that reflects the mystical source of that tradition. This happens with atheists, agnostics, religious Christians and Jews, Catholics-turned-Buddhist, Jews-turned-Sufi, shamanic practitioners, and any other combination one might consider. Why does this occur and what does it mean? This is the central focus of the book. I will show that in the souls of people born into the Judeo-Christian tradition, there is a deep truth and vitality. This truth and vitality is there for the purpose of their own spiritual development and for the development of Western culture as well. The problem, however, is that far too many of these people reject such a possibility.

Our Spiritual Contradiction

Life in America seems to be spiraling out of control. From the unremitting stories of war, terrorism and suffering, to the threat of worldwide economic collapse and the clash of cultural ideologies at home, we are experiencing unprecedented levels of psychological stress in our lives. Violence has become epidemic. Sexual abuse and rape claim nearly a quarter of our children. Almost one in four adults suffers from a diagnosed mental disorder, such as anxiety, depression, eating disorders, post-traumatic stress, attention-deficit disorders, bipolar disorder, suicide, schizophrenia, and an assortment of syndromes, phobias and personality problems.[1] Use of antidepressants, sleeping aids and anti-anxiety medication has become the norm. In a given year, according to the most recent study from the National Institute of

Mental Health (NIMH), the numbers of people affected add up to 57.7 million people.[2] The effects of mental illness, including suicide, on health and productivity in America has long been underestimated. It accounts for more than 15 percent of all diseases—more than the disease burden caused by cancer.[3]

In contrast with this evidence of cultural breakdown, we have a recent major survey by the esteemed Pew Forum on Religion and Public Life, which revealed that ninety-two percent of Americans report a belief in God or in a "Higher Power."[4] A look at the publishing industry shows that books about personal growth and spirituality continue to capture a large segment of the market, which has been the case for decades. Such widespread attention to spiritual matters should be having a beneficial effect on our culture. But this does not seem to be true.

A closer look at spirituality in the West gives a sense of the problem. The search for meaning, which is so crucial for psychological health, has lost its traditional anchors. Millions of people are going it alone, creating their own belief systems. Visit any dating website and note that the majority of profiles have checked the category "spiritual but not religious" (SBNR). According to a 2012 Pew report, almost 1 in 5 Americans are in this group.[5] It points to the diversity of the individual search today.

This shift began back in the sixties, as people left traditional religion and began exploring Eastern traditions like Buddhism, Hinduism, and Sufism, as well as different forms of nature worship, including shamanism, Native American spirituality, and Wicca.[6] Both Jews and Christians in the West have followed this trend, which means that the age-old divide in belief systems between Jews and non-Jews is narrowing, especially among adults aged 35 and younger.[7] In contrast with this trend, another percentage of the population has increasingly embraced conservative Christianity—from around 200,000 in 1990 to more than 8 million today.

Such contradictions demonstrate the many complex factors around the topic of the spiritual life in the West. Clearly we have reached a pivotal moment, where so many negative forces seem to be pulling us apart, even while many powerful forces for the good, especially seen through rapidly growing global communication, are bringing people around the world ever closer together.

What then, is the essential issue that is causing so much angst and suffering? My strong belief is that too many people are unable to find answers to their deepest questions, either in today's religious institutions, or through the spiritual smorgasbord that has infiltrated Western culture and is readily available through books, workshops, and media.

The Hunger for Spiritual Guidance

In spite of all the ambivalence and angst around religion, spirituality, and personal wellbeing in today's popular culture, I always bring the theme of spiritual development into the psychology courses I teach. The reason is that I don't believe there can be growth and development without the spiritual component. This perspective has earned appreciation and recognition from students. They are hungry for guidance about how to stay centered in our uncertain, stressful times.

One of the projects in my course on childhood development was for students to write a "spiritual autobiography," recounting any of their early childhood experiences of spiritual connection. They regularly wrote about their visions and premonitions or feelings of contact from a sacred reality. Over the years, I have been continually disheartened and saddened to read about times of spiritual opening, faith and inspiration, only to hear how the meaning of such experiences disappeared, and then the subsequent struggles to find meaning in times of turmoil. Here are some comments not only from my psychology students, but from my adult clients as well.

From Students:

- Marcia: *Up until the age of nine, I would experience regular dream visitations from my grandmother, who had died when I was six. I loved her and missed her desperately but was forbidden to talk about her and my visions. Instead, I was put on anti-depressants.*

- Evan: *How can I believe in a God after the Holocaust? I have no faith in anything. I often feel scared about death and the future. Life seems to be just a matter of luck, and that is really unfair.*

- Clarissa: *I am not an atheist. I don't know what I am. My parents were Protestant, but did not have me baptized because they wanted to give me the freedom to come to my own decisions about religion. But I'm still searching for a sign that will show me where to begin. I have overwhelming fears about the idea that there is nothing at all after death. Although I try to convince myself that I may be reincarnated into another being, this belief does not give me any security. I am consumed by the fear that life is all there is, and after that, there is nothing.*

From clients:

- Jack: *Even though I was abused by a priest when I was an altar boy, I remained in the church and still believe in God. The influences from childhood are so deep that I am afraid to go it alone. All the same, I don't say anything about beliefs to my children. My wife is an atheist, which divides our family so that we never talk about anything meaningful. When my six-year-old asked me about death, I just avoided the subject.*

- Suzanne: *We went to church infrequently, yet my parents encouraged us to think about God and to regularly pray. After going through the women's movement, I didn't't want to have anything to do with the patriarchy in Christianity, so now I just meet every now and then with friends and we debate issues like whether there is a God. I always leave feeling that we never get close to any answers.*

- Jackie: *I have been active in a variety of spiritual groups and communities. During one group, I participated in a trance dance where we would contact a Higher power. During this dance, I once became sort of manic and had to be hospitalized. Now I'm afraid to believe anything and can't function without lithium. I struggle all the time with depression.*

Lost Moorings

Such stories illustrate the crux of the issue that concerns me so deeply. People are rejecting traditional religion—often understandably—because it doesn't support their spiritual yearnings, or because of its historical abuses, or because it feels outdated and meaningless. Yet in many respects, these seekers are rootless. There is a crucial piece missing in their search. It has to do with what it means to be born in the Western world. Opening to our Judeo-Christian roots allows us to be nourished by the Western mystical ground. This ground is our birthright. It means to have a direct connection with the Higher Power, to acknowledge and make choices between good and evil, to practice unconditional love, humility, and forgiveness. As I'll explain, these are actual, innate forces in us that have to do with the deep spiritual/cultural undercurrents in a person's soul. Neither spiritual development nor spiritual identities are extraneous factors in the human condition. They are central. They are deeply serious issues for mental and emotional health and wellbeing.

There is another concern. A spiritual search is very often about opening to different levels of consciousness. This can sometimes lead to powerful inner states, such as voices, visions, and dreams. Moreover, such experiences can happen completely spontaneously, whether the individual is a spiritual seeker or not.

The mainstream mental health interpretation is that such experiences are either a fantasy, meaningless, or indicative of mental illness. In this book, I share my belief that these are deeply meaningful messages that relate to the soul's desire for healing. Part One of this book looks at the healing function of the soul and then examines how our three primary support systems—religion, psychology, and the New Age movement—leave millions of people adrift by denying or misunderstanding authentic Western spirituality.

In Part Two, I share definitions of God and talk about the important influence of our Western mystical roots. I contrast some differences between the Western and the Eastern mindset and explain why, unlike in the East, we need to make conscious choices between good and evil, rather than call them illusory. Finally, I share ways that I combine spirituality with psychological development for personal growth and healing.

Part Three outlines a three-stage model of the Western path of spiritual development, based on the age-old writings of Western mystics. I talk about the types of experiences that occur in each stage, their characteristics, specific psycho-spiritual challenges, and how countless people throughout the ages have followed the same path to Union—more commonly known as Enlightenment.

It is important for me to acknowledge that I approach the many topics in this book as an experiencer, witness, and facilitator. I have learned by doing, questioning, and exploring. I can only say that my message comes from a life spent immersed in an extraordinary field of spiritual wisdom available to us all.

There are many heroes and heroines in the following pages. They are clients and students who have found the courage to question our culture's postmodern and secular view of the human journey. As they have discovered, this path, while challenging, allows them to realize what it means to be fully alive.

PART ONE

OUR WESTERN SPIRITUAL ANGST

CHAPTER 1

TWO WAYS OF KNOWING

*I do not myself grasp all that I am. Thus the mind is
too narrow to contain itself.
But where can that part be which it does not contain?*

—St. Augustine (354-430 C.E.)

*Our normal waking consciousness, rational
consciousness as we call it, is but one special type
of consciousness, whilst all about it, parted from it
by the filmiest of screens, there lie potential forms of
consciousness entirely different.*

—William James (1902)

Not long ago, I received a phone call from a 24-year-old college
student I'll call Craig. He told me he been interested in spirituality for several years, had read many books on the subject, and
had been participating in a series of meditation classes for several months. During one of his meditations, he had a dramatic
out-of-body experience, saw blinding light, and felt the presence
of angels. Then, he had a vision of his father (who had died when

Craig was young) and he was flooded with feelings of love. "I walked around for five days afterwards, smiling at everyone," he told me. "I felt clear, open to everyone, and able to love unconditionally."

Craig told me that his "crown chakra," (the energy center at the top of the head, described in Hindu spirituality and known to practitioners of yoga) was still tingling, as was his "third eye," (the energy center between the eyebrows). But he was not calling because he wanted to talk about his spiritual opening, but because of what had happened next.

Craig's feelings of bliss were followed by paranoia and a psychotic breakdown. He had frightening dreams where he was pursued by demons. He imagined that his neighbors were spying on him and he accused his college roommates of conspiring to hurt him. Unnerved by Craig's strange behavior, all three roommates moved out, leaving him isolated and afraid.

Craig's meditation teacher was unable to provide him with assistance or assurance, and gave him the name of a psychiatrist affiliated with Craig's university counseling center. His mother was notified about his state of mind and she and the counseling center arranged to have him committed to a mental hospital, where he spent five days. He was released with a regimen of anti-psychotic drugs and began regular sessions with a psychologist and a body worker.

In spite of all this support, Craig was still having trouble. He had the initiative and where-with-all, however, to research his breakdown, which led him to call me. After hearing his story, I asked him how his relationship with his professional helpers was working out. Craig replied that he had stopped taking the anti-psychotics and had been told by the body worker that all he really needed was some "energy release."

"That's not going to really help you," I said. "The good news is that you seem to be an aware and psychologically sophisticated person. If you want to come to terms with your experiences, however, you need to understand that they contained important messages about yourself and your life."

"I felt so loved and powerful," Craig said. "I don't understand why everything turned around like that."

"It is not possible for you to find those answers now," I replied. "You must deal with your 'baggage' to put it in popular terms, or what Carl Jung, the influential Swiss psychiatrist (1875-1961), called the shadow self.[7a] The shadow refers to those uncomfortable parts of our nature that we repress, such as fear, anger, jealousy and greed. A powerful spiritual experience like yours can be so transformative and emotionally disruptive, that it will cause unresolved issues in a person's life to surface. Darkness comes with light, and you experienced both very dramatically. Unless you are willing to face and work through what those issues are about, you will be unable to use what you've been given. It takes courage, but it is the most worthwhile thing you can possibly do for your life."

Why Do-It-Yourself Spirituality Doesn't Work

It is not unusual for people to report some sort of emotional upheaval triggered through meditative practice, although it is not always as traumatic as that which Craig experienced. As he and I talked, I learned that he had grown up in a home with atheist parents who discounted the spiritual aspects of existence with a combination of science and pragmatism. He, however, was introspective by nature, hungry for different answers, and believed that education and meditation would provide an opportunity to explore some of his questions. As such, he was like an explorer out in the wilds without any clear idea of what he was looking for, or what he should do about whatever he encountered.

For thousands of years, people have known that opening consciousness to a reality greater than the individual self is an integral part of a spiritual practice. The result of Craig's questing, however, is an all-too-common example of what can occur today. Many people who are creating their own spiritual path have trouble realizing what is happening and that their spiritual search might very well catapult them into unknown territory.

"The higher you go on levels of reality, the deeper you go in your own selfhood," says the great religious scholar Huston Smith. "You face your soul, and become aware of who you really are and of what is truly important in life."[8] When Craig began to meditate, neither he nor his meditation teacher realized where his experiences would lead. They were, in fact awakening him to his spiritual nature. Sadly, he ended up with an array of people who wanted to restore him to his former reality. He was working with a psychologist, with a body worker who was trying to rebalance his energy, and taking drugs to alter his brain chemistry.

Each of these approaches was trying to help, but each was failing to address the fact that there was deep and important meaning in what Craig had experienced.

Craig's Experience Was About Healing

The great physician and humanitarian Albert Schweitzer (1875—1965) wrote, "No one can give a definition of the soul. But we know what it feels like. The soul is the sense of something higher than ourselves, something that stirs in us thoughts, hopes, and aspirations which go out to the world of goodness, truth and beauty. The soul is a burning desire to breathe in this world of light and never to lose it—to remain children of light."[9]

Many people today will have trouble defining or explaining the existence of God, but few will deny the reality of their soul. They may not be able to define what soul is; nevertheless, most will vehemently defend its existence as the source of their deepest truth.

I believe that when psychology discounts the power of the soul, it loses its ability to provide real guidance and healing.

All of Craig's experiences were messages from the deepest part of his being that required attention. First, through the experience of blinding light, the presence of angels, the vision of his father and the feelings of love, he was experiencing his true nature, as a spiritual being in a physical body. Second, he was being shown that love is eternal and that his father was still present and connected to him. Third, he was given information on what he needed to "fix" in order to become whole and free of pain and shadow.

This makes extraordinary sense. The human body knows how to heal itself from a physical wound; why would we not also have an innate ability to heal from our psychological and emotional wounds?

Craig still had unresolved pain concerning the loss of his father at such a young age. It had been buried deep and never dealt with. As a result, it resulted in anger, grief, a sense of abandonment and a fear of death and the unknown. Giving Craig medication only suppressed his unresolved angst. He needed guidance and support to access the knowledge of unconditional love that transcends death, an energy that had always been there from his father. This would be his anchor as he began the process of dealing with his shadow. In his case, this meant that he had to deal with the repressed feelings of abandonment, rage, and fear he had carried since his father had disappeared from his life. As we mature spiritually, the more light we access, the more shadow surfaces to show us what work remains.

This is why I say that both spiritual and psychological development are one and the same. There cannot be one without the other.

Being human means that we need to remember that we are not separate from the energetic processes of life and death. These processes include creativity, growth, change, and transformation. For me, as a developmental psychologist, this is a powerful realization. From the physical to the most ineffable parts of our natures, we grow and develop in the same way, from seed to flower to fruit. *We are born whole. If we are injured, our natural impulse is always in the direction of healing and becoming whole again.* Even at the end of life, when the body is breaking down, the soul is still growing. It informs everything. It contains nature, but is beyond nature, connecting us with the great mystery of being.

This means that the important point is that it's not about a psychotherapist, rabbi, priest, minister, or New Age guru finding the cure. *Our own cure is built in already.* Many have lost sight of this essential truth.

The Other Voice Within

How then does the soul relate to the ego? Carl Jung distinguished between a person's "small self" (the ego), which is reflected in our individual personality, and a "Higher Self" (the soul) through which we contact and express the energy of God.[10] Clearly, there is a big difference between these two parts of our nature. Each has its own way of knowing, a concept both ancient and universal.

Some examples from teachers and philosophers across the centuries, are cited in *The Spectrum of Consciousness* by contemporary writer and philosopher Ken Wilber.[11]

- Daybreak knowledge versus Twilight Knowledge (Meister Eckhart, 12th century mystic and theologian);
- Lower Knowing versus Higher Knowing (Hinduism);
- Knowing Conceptually versus Knowing Intuitively

(William   James,   19th   century   psychologist   and
philosopher);

• Thought versus Awareness (Krishnamurti, 19th century
philosopher); and

• Dual versus Non-dual consciousness (Ken Wilber).[12]

The ego is the master in the small self, a vast intellectual and
cultural construct that manages our daily concerns. It controls
our individuality, personality, our role, power, popularity, and
financial and social successes or failures in life. Its way of knowing processes information from the five senses as well as values
and beliefs that we assume from popular culture and make our
own.

Through the soul we experience our true nature and identity. Soul knowledge can be immanent or transcendent, arising
within or from beyond the self. It comes through consciousness,
in dreams, hearing voices, sounds, music, or there can be visions,
such as blinding light. There can also be unexpected and inexplicable insights pertaining to our lives and futures, and even
reality itself. There can be intuitions, such as the sudden awareness that a loved one is in trouble. It may be precognitive, such
as thinking of a person two seconds before he or she calls on the
phone, or startling synchronicities, where one's inner world can
be witnessed in external reality. I'll say more about such experiences in the next chapter.

In the West, we are encouraged by our institutions and
experts to develop strong egos, to be in control of our lives, to
be rational, active, and independent. Such an individualistic

perspective puts us in competition with everyone else and requires that we think about ourselves as separate, with definite boundaries between self and others. In fact, psychology considers such boundaries imperative.

What we fail to recognize is that ego is basically human-made and finite. But soul belongs to a boundless and eternal dimension. This is why Plato said of soul knowledge, "Heaven-sent madness is superior to man-made sanity."[12a] When my clients talk to me about their experiences from soul, they most often say, "It was the most real experience I've ever had." Soul knowledge changes lives.

Psychology calls this soul-knowledge intuition or insight, but the problem is that psychology *only* credits the individual with the knowing, not realizing that it is not the individual's personality, intelligence, or "goodness" that brings such knowledge about. Rather, it is the Sacred or the God force, what some call consciousness that comes through the individual (a full discussion about God in section two). Why do we consider it real? Because of the powerful effects of spiritual experiences on people who have them.

Why Spiritual Experiences Cannot be Ignored

"The way most people first discover consciousness is through some form of spiritual experience," writes contemporary philosopher and spiritual teacher Andrew Cohen. "I'm talking about the momentous occasion when someone stumbles for the first time upon that miraculous dimension of the self that transcends memory and time, that deepest part of ourselves where there is no cognition, there is only Being. This discovery leaves a permanent mark on our souls."[13]

No other experience can be so transformative. This is why it is essential that the psychology field recognize its power.

The main purpose of psychotherapy today is to help people understand the source of feelings and behaviors that are having a negative impact on their lives, and to find ways to change the pattern. Without a doubt, this is helpful and important. Many practitioners in mental health centers begin by doing an "intake interview" and filling out a form that identifies the "presenting problem and psychiatric diagnosis." One of the biggest problems with such an approach, however, is that the focus is on pathology.

For example, while it is understandable that Craig's psychiatrist was interested in his unresolved father issues, there was a problem when Craig's spiritual experiences were not acknowledged. Not only were his extreme fears not dealt with, but his light-filled visions and experiences of love were also ignored. Psychotherapy will too often call such experiences delusional and an indication of some glitch in the brain. With such a model, the focus of Craig's psychotherapy would only be about working through feelings of anger and abandonment. Such an approach will not strengthen his heart and soul, nor will it help him grapple with the meaning of death and his life purpose.

Providing "Treatment" versus Supporting a Process

One of the most important distinctions between the psycho-spiritual work I engage in, and mainstream psychotherapy is the role assumed by the professional. Since I am not providing treatment, I instead function as a witness and a facilitator to something that is unfolding, or attempting to evolve, within my client. I come from the perspective that we are born whole— body and soul. And if we are injured, our natural impulse is always in the direction of healing and becoming whole again. Synchronicities, dreams, life events, all have meaning. They are not random occurrences, but messages for growth and development. Thus, my work is not to diagnose and treat a person, but to support what is trying to come forth through the soul.

I call this unfolding a "process." One of the definitions for process is "natural outgrowth." I assume that we are each in a natural, meaningful process throughout life. Thus, when one of my clients describes something that is happening in his or her life, I usually ask, "Well, what is your process telling you?"

When I worked with Craig, I began with his spiritual experiences. I asked him what they meant to him. I asked him to consider why he had felt such overwhelming love coming from his father. I affirmed the light, the visions, the angels, and the totality of the experience. I emphasized that it was important to take it very seriously.

Why did I do this first? Psycho-spiritual work has two goals: to encourage people to access the wisdom of their soul and to offer support so that the person can trust and follow its guidance. As psychologist, spiritual guide, and facilitator, I am working with multiple levels of awareness, both examining thoughts and feelings and also acknowledging the power of our two ways of knowing. Such a combination guides the client towards a new way of being.

I believed that Craig's soul was craving spiritual connection and nourishment. This is why he began to meditate in the first place. When he expanded his consciousness through meditation, that nourishment came flooding in, confirming that he was not separate from God, and that his father was still present, loving, and available to him in his life. This could have been an extraordinary and immensely powerful realization, but he had no real help, even from his meditation teacher, to help him accept and integrate this message into his life. Thus, although he was initially in a state of gratitude and bliss, his unresolved shadow quickly emerged and took him in the other direction, into fears that he was going crazy, and eventually into paranoia.

This is a perfect example of how soul knowledge is denied in today's world. Craig's psychologist was under the impression that Craig's spiritual experience was solely an unresolved psychological issue about his father. Unless Craig could be helped to fully understand the spiritual message from his soul, all psychotherapeutic attempts to work out his father issues would fail.

Sometimes a client may respond to me by saying the spiritual experience is only a figment of the imagination. Given our society's prevailing worldviews, this is not surprising. In such cases, and as long as the client is willing, I don't give up. I continue to show the person how important such experiences are for learning the truth of human nature. One way may be through dream exploration; another through a method that expands consciousness, such as Breathwork.

People must understand that our soul connects us to a higher spiritual reality. This connection is innate, not human-made. A person will go through life always adrift, unable to be sure about anything, diminished and unwise, when this connection is not known.

CHAPTER 2

A CRACK BETWEEN THE WORLDS

*There is a theory which states that if ever anybody
discovers exactly what the Universe is for and why it
is here, it will instantly disappear and be replaced by
something even more bizarre and inexplicable. There
is another theory which states that this has already
happened.*

——Douglas Adams (1980)

My deep interest in psychology and spiritual development stems
from the numerous times I have had my own dramatic expansion of consciousness. I had a secular upbringing; thus, my background cannot explain my spiritual experiences. I was born and
grew up in the Philadelphia suburbs with my lawyer father, my
stay-at-home mother, and a younger brother. We were members
of a synagogue and went to services on the important Jewish
holidays. My brother and I also went to Hebrew school and my
parents belonged to the temple's social organizations. In spite of
these activities, our family's religiosity was much like the nature

of contemporary Judaism at that time, meaning that we were more oriented to social, traditional, cultural, and community considerations than anything that had to do with cultivating a personal relationship with God.

From childhood, however, I seemed to be inclined toward a deep inner life. For example, at the age of seven, there was my spontaneous and passionate prayer to God to heal my brother after I heard my parents worry that he might have polio. Another time, I had a precognitive dream of a surprise birthday party that came true on the following day, down to the last detail. And, as I grew to adulthood, I felt an abiding sense that there was something "out there" for me to know and experience beyond the traditional structures of my life, marriage and career.

My first and quite shocking out-of-body experience took place when I was a young adult. I was employed as a clinical counselor at Horizon House, a psychiatric rehabilitation center in Philadelphia for individuals with diagnoses of psychosis and schizophrenia. I was especially interested in my clients' inner experiences, which all seemed to be centered on the same theme. This theme had to do with the powerful icons in our Western spiritual heritage, such as God, Jesus, Mary, or the Devil. I wondered why my profession did not take their clients' states of consciousness seriously, given that they seemed to occur in so many of the people who have a diagnosis of serious mental illness. The field of psychiatry even came up with the term "religious ideation" as evidence that they also recognized this phenomenon. And yet, they had no interest in exploring why all these people were having such experiences. Almost every person I worked with seemed to be caught in a spiritual struggle between light and darkness.

I was particularly drawn to Frederick, a forty-something man with a very striking appearance of sparkling blue eyes, bright red hair, and a full mustache. Early on in our therapeutic relationship, he told me about a childhood vision he had at the age of seven while walking home from school. He suddenly heard a voice calling to him, saying, "Young Frederick, look up at the sky!"

He looked up. There was the Virgin Mary, surrounded by a brilliant white light and holding the baby Jesus in her arms. He heard Jesus say to him, "I will be with you, young Frederick, for the rest of your life."

Frederick ran home to tell his mother. She was alarmed by his story and took him to a psychiatrist, who put him on antipsychotic medication. Frederick was forbidden to speak of his experience ever again.

After a rocky childhood, Frederick ended up spending his adult life in supervised living facilities and attending partial hospitalization day programs. I met him through one of the latter. When I heard his story, I was very curious and asked him how Jesus appeared to him now. I was struck by his response; he replied, "Jesus doesn't look like others describe Him. He has bright red hair, a full mustache, and sparkling blue eyes."

I could not help but wonder if, at some level, Frederick understood that he was describing himself. It is very common for people with a diagnosis of psychosis to catapult into a state of spiritual consciousness without being grounded enough to handle the experience. They make their experience literal, and then, they do not know how to integrate their visions into their identity and everyday lives. Because Frederick's entire life had been focused around his childhood spiritual experience, and because he had never had a therapist who accepted its validity, the only way he could understand it was to literally live it and act it out. Just like the pre-verbal child, who can only show rather than tell, Frederick's whole life had become a drama about a question that no one would help him answer.

As I listened to details about my clients' spiritual experiences, I asked them what they thought they meant. They were shy at first. No other psychotherapist had ever asked about such things before. And then, they were deeply grateful for my interest, since their experiences were their most powerful and important reality. Yet not only was my profession dismissive, it was using medication to actively suppress those experiences.

These are the basic labels given to such episodes of expanded consciousness:

Subjective—not based in fact, related to personal feelings and opinions;

Coincidence—an accidental event that seems preplanned;

Imagination, Fantasy—a wishful product of the mind;

Delusion—a belief without any basis in consensus reality;

Hallucination—a false sense-perception of objects or events;

Psychosis—a mental break with consensus reality;

Religious ideation—psychotic religious experiences.

Most of us are familiar with these descriptions. Such labels have a power that denies our ability to explore and fully embrace our spiritual nature and soul knowledge. As a result, many people are not sure what their spiritual experience means. Is it a mere belief or something real? Is it a sign of mental instability, wishful thinking, a fantasy, or a religious dogma?

The more I spent time with my clients, the more I began to feel that the labels "delusion," "hallucination," and "religious ideation" were bypassing something that was much more profound. I was often assigned the most challenging clients who were openly talking about their inner spiritual conflicts and struggles. I continued to observe that they felt affirmed when they realized I was taking their experiences seriously. Some, after being able to express themselves fully, showed that they felt much better and calmer. I remember a patient named Tony saying to me, "Judith, thanks for letting me know that I don't have to be a victim and follow that evil voice in my head that keeps telling me to hurt myself. I can tell it that I will not listen—and then pray to my angel to protect me and help me be strong." Tony was not an isolated case, but becoming the norm. I was feeling certain that my clients' spiritual experiences were deep inner struggles that symbolized the light and dark aspects of being human.

"Epiphenomena"

During this time period I had an experience one night as I was falling asleep that was life changing. As I lay drowsing in bed, I suddenly became aware of a relentless tugging sensation on my right side. I felt as if my soul, my essence, was about to fly out of my body. In fact, I felt that if it did, I would die. During those same moments I heard a strange and unknown word inside my head. It was coming from the left side of my brain: "Epiphenomena, epiphenomena, epiphenomena, epiphenomena. . ."

I had no control over my body, my consciousness, or my identity. I was terrified. I could not move, cry out, or put an end to the chaos in my mind.

Meanwhile, my husband Marty slept peacefully by my side. Whether this extraordinary event went on for a minute or for hours, I could not guess. The experience was beyond time. And then suddenly it was over. I don't know why then I did not get out of bed, turn on the light, or even waken Marty. Instead, I turned over and fell into a deep sleep.

When I woke the following morning, I felt too weak to get out of bed but managed to tell Marty about the unknown word "epiphenomena." By 4:00 in the afternoon I felt like myself. At dinnertime, as we spoke further, Marty suggested we look up the definition of "epiphenomena." It turned out to be a real word, and represented the way that psychology and psychiatry make sense of peoples' expanded states of consciousness and spiritual experiences: "a secondary mental phenomenon caused by . . . a physical phenomenon, *but [which] has no causal influence itself.*"[14]

Just as the psychology field refers to such experiences as hallucinations and delusions, so would it interpret my experience the same way—a mere chemical misfire of the brain.

My heart began pounding as I abruptly realized that *epiphenomena* summarized the increasing tension in my life between my soul and the scientific worldview of clinical psychology. And suddenly, in that moment of revelation, there was a loud bang that shook the house, as if the abrupt realization was so powerful, it had opened a crack between the worlds. I was completely stunned and unable to react. Marty heard the sound, our two young children began to cry in fear, and our dog began to bark. Here I was, a young, happily married woman, with children and a meaningful career, and now what? I could not ignore what was happening to me. I just knew, deep down, that I wasn't mentally ill. I continued to work as a counselor and began studying for a Ph.D.

More spiritual experiences occurred, sometimes feeling sacred, sometimes surreal, and sometimes quite crazy. I began to research mystical literature and altered states of consciousness. It seemed that my experiences were very similar to those of my clients. Yet somehow, for some reason, I was considered emotionally healthy and they were not.

Carl Jung, who founded the school of Analytical Psychology, coined the term "collective unconscious." He wrote:

> In addition to our immediate consciousness, which is of a thoroughly personal nature, there exists a second psychic system of a collective, universal and impersonal nature which is identical in all individuals. This collective unconscious does not develop individually but is inherited.[14a]

He gained much of his perspective on the collective unconscious through his own spiritual journey and through his work with patients. It felt affirming to read that he believed that a shift in therapeutic focus from pathology to the "numinous" (from the Latin *numen*, meaning "the active power of the divine")[15] was central in healing:

> The approach to the numinous is the real therapy, and inasmuch you attune to the numinous experiences you are released from the curse of pathology. Even the very disease takes on a numinous character.[16]

This was an extraordinary point of view, that the so-called "mental illness" was actually spiritual in nature, and not psychopathology. To me, this meant that psychotherapy could, and should, be about supporting a person through a "spiritual crisis" rather than management of symptoms. What if the mental health profession had got it all wrong? What if the very key to helping clients lay in working to understand what their voices, visions, and dreams were actually about?

Discovering Why Psychology Needs Spirituality

I received a Ph.D. in psychology and began to teach at the college level. I also began to work at Matrix Research Institute, a non-profit research and development "think tank" that received government grants for training mental health professionals who worked with seriously mentally ill clients. I developed curricula, trained mental health professionals, and consulted with the National Institute of Mental Health in Washington, D.C. I also engaged in private psychotherapy with my own clients.

While the work I was doing was exciting in many ways, I was also frustrated that the disciplines of psychology and psychiatry continually interpreted personal spiritual experience as a marker of mental illness. The more I worked with my clients, the more intensely I felt about this issue. I became active in the International Association of Near-Death Studies (IANDS) and counseled people who had near-death and other mystical experiences. It became more and more clear. Their stories, my stories, and the stories of my psychiatric clients were all tapping into the same energies.

I began to really trust my perceptions, which were so different from those of my colleagues. At the same time my own spiritual experiences were getting stronger, more frequent, and often confusing. I decided to seek my own psychotherapy because I was feeling increasingly torn between the accepted beliefs of the psychology field and my new, growing, spiritual worldview. My heart kept telling me that I needed to find a way to bring psychology and spirituality together. I had no idea what this meant.

My therapist, who was a highly respected psychiatrist, listened to me without expression. Then he suggested we explore my relationship with my parents. As I tried over and over to tell him about my spiritual experiences, and my conflicts with my profession, he became more and more uncomfortable, saying, "I don't deal with the sorts of things you are talking about."

I quit after some months, feeling lost, confused, and alone as I left his office. Where was I to go, and what was I to do now? And then, the very next day, I received an announcement in the mail from Dr. Stanislav Grof about a three-year intensive training program in consciousness studies for mental health professionals. The focus was on learning about different states of consciousness, going through the process called Holotropic Breathwork (previously mentioned), and learning how to work with clients using this same approach.

Working Therapeutically With Different States of Consciousness

Dr. Grof was a Czech psychiatrist and pioneer in consciousness exploration, and had been living and working in the US since the 1960's. He created Holotropic Breathwork with his wife Christina, as a practice that expands consciousness through a combination of deep meditation accompanied by powerful inspirational music.

When I began the training, I had already been having spontaneous experiences of expanded consciousness for years. However, I never fully understood that perhaps they might have a purpose for my life. So although I had a sense that they were important and in some way part of my life path, I had not known how to put everything together. I felt that Breathwork could be a way for me to learn more about what was unfolding in me. It also would deepen my understanding of what was going on with my clients, including those with a diagnosis of mental illness.

The training program gave me a spiritual guide in Stan Grof for the first time in my life. Initially I was unsure about intentionally opening up with a group of strangers. But then, over the months, as the Breathwork took me deeper and deeper into my soul, I realized that I was safe and that every experience of expanded consciousness led me into a much clearer understanding of myself.

As I was nearing the end of my time with Grof and my fellow participants, I realized that I had reached a crossroads. During this period, I was still training mental health professionals at Matrix, but it was becoming evident that I no longer believed in the treatment methods I was teaching. My experiences both in and out of Breathwork were increasingly spiritual, including visions of Jesus similar to those of Western saints and mystics. As I began to lead my own Breathwork groups, my clients also seemed to be having similar experiences. How could a Jewish woman like me be having religious visions that had no connection to my birth religion? While very meaningful overall, my Breathwork training had not provided me with a satisfactory explanation. I felt vulnerable and very much alone.

I headed for a library and began to wander through the stacks, not even clear where I was going to find an answer. Then, I came across a book published in 1911 and titled *Mysticism: A Study of the Nature and Development of Man's Spiritual Consciousness,* written by a British woman named Evelyn Underhill (1875-1941). She described a five-stage path of spiritual development that she called "The Mystic Way," which Western mystics and saints have been traveling for thousands of years.

I still remember the initial surprise, growing excitement, and pure joy I felt as I began to read Underhill's work. Because she was English, her early 20th century writing style was not easy to read. Nonetheless, she seemed to be describing down to the last detail what I was experiencing in my own inner world, which at the time was shocking, perplexing, and very difficult for me to accept or to integrate. Not only did Underhill's book describe and confirm what was happening with me, it paralleled my perceptions of the types of processes I was witnessing in many of my clients. It also confirmed that my responses to them were appropriate.

When today I am asked to name my most important spiritual teacher, I can easily say it was Evelyn Underhill. It is hard to put into words how grateful I am for her monumental labor of scholarly expertise and dedication. Through *Mysticism,* she gave me information that supported my own inner world. It also acted as a map and a guidebook that I could consult when I was unclear, afraid, or lacked confidence in myself, in my clients, and sometimes even in God.

Mysticism is the Wellspring

Mysticism comes first. Religion is the offspring. While an experience of expanded consciousness might include a surprising synchronicity or a significant dream, a mystical experience reveals the core of existence. Said Underhill:

> Mysticism in its pure form is the science of the Ultimate. The science of Union with the Absolute and nothing else, and *the mystic is the person who attains this Union, not the person who talks about it* (my emphasis). Not to know about, but to Be, is the mark of the real initiate.[17]

A scholar of Western spiritual consciousness, and a mystic herself, Underhill described mysticism as "the hunger for reality, the unwillingness to be satisfied with the purely animal or the purely social level of consciousness."[18] In other words, she understood that mystics see the Source, the true reality, from behind the veil of our material world.

It was after I discovered Underhill's work that the split between my professional identity and my opening to spirituality began to heal. As I avidly read her work and became familiar with the writings of other Western mystics and saints, I gained a much better understanding of the many ups and downs of my own path and the paths of my clients. This required a big shift in my thinking. I could now clearly see the difference between the work I was starting to do with my clients, and that of my profession.

My passion became to influence the way mental health is practiced in our culture. The kind of success I was having with many of my clients showed me that I had discovered something immensely important. I felt in the depths of my being that psychology needed spirituality and that many who were diagnosed psychotic were actually having spiritual crises instead. Such people would be so much better served were there a wise spiritual elder to support and guide them, rather than a doctor with a prescription pad.

The Mystical Experience of Eckhart Tolle

As I've already said, and will discuss further in the next chapter, there is much about spiritual experience that can be confusing, disturbing, and worrisome to the status quo, even though for many people, especially those who are spiritual seekers, it can be a life-changing and deeply important event. Such experiences are not to be feared or denied. The problem is not the experience. It is the lack of support and understanding in our culture for such events.

A powerful dream or a surprising synchronicity can be fairly easily incorporated into the lives of most people who experience them. Some of the experiences that I have been talking about are not so easily integrated because they are so powerful. They can take over a person's life. A recent example is the life story of world-renowned, bestselling author of *The Power of Now* Eckhart Tolle, who contemplated suicide in his twenties after a deep and prolonged depression. As he lay in bed in the early morning with the thought of self-annihilation, he suddenly had a deeply mystical revelation about the power of the present moment. In fact, it was so powerful, it took over his entire being. He writes:

> I felt drawn into what seemed like a vortex of energy. . . I was gripped by an intense fear and my body started to shake. I could feel myself being sucked into a void. It felt as if the void was inside me rather than outside. Suddenly, there was no more fear and I let myself fall into that void. I have no recollection of what happened after that.[19]

When Tolle came back to himself, all of his senses were heightened and the world had become intensely beautiful and vividly alive. He writes, "That day I walked around the city in utter amazement at the miracle of life on earth, as if I had just been born into this world."[20]

And then, for the next five months, he says, "I lived in a state of uninterrupted deep peace and bliss."[21] Tolle eventually learned to go into the timeless realm that he had experienced and remain conscious. His experiences of bliss intensified beyond even what he had originally experienced. What is especially important for this chapter, however, is this next part in his story:

> A time came when, for a while, I was left with nothing on the physical plane. I had no relationships, no job, no home, and no socially defined identity. I spent almost two years sitting on park benches in a state of the most intense joy.[22]

Tolle was fortunate; he had enough grounding in philosophy and spirituality, plus a natural curiosity about the inner life. He did not run off to a psychiatrist for medication to stop what was happening to him. And although he does not say in his book how he survived, he must have had some sort of support system to keep him alive. Yet it's clear that most people witnessing his state during that time would have diagnosed that mental illness was occurring and not a spiritual process.

Tolle's experiences led to an extraordinarily powerful message about the power of the present moment. His book has sold millions of copies around the world. Much inner work had to be done in order for him to become a teacher for so many people and, as I have said, he had already spent years studying and reading in philosophy and spirituality. By contrast, the following story of my student Mark was different. Mark had no grounding when his experience occurred in, of all places, a New York subway.

Mark's Premature State of Union

Of Christian Spanish decent, Mark was raised in a non-religious family, but grew up with an interest in spirituality. He had never actively explored it until he took my class on spiritual development. As the semester progressed, I became aware that he seemed motivated to fully open himself for the first time in his life to a psycho-spiritual worldview. It turned out that once Mark became responsive, his soul showed him what was possible.

Mark left work as usual, and headed for the long commute home on the subway. As the doors closed, he suddenly and unexpectedly was propelled into an expanded state of spiritual consciousness. He felt enveloped by an invisible and loving force. At the same time, he became vividly aware of each of the many commuters on the train. He seemed to be able to see everyone in great detail, including their stance, their clothing, and what they were carrying. He also could intensely feel their inner states. He actually had the feeling that he was merged with each and every person in the subway. And not only did he feel merged, he also experienced that everyone was linked with one another. "We were all One," said Mark.

This ecstatic state of consciousness strengthened with another vision of a white mist moving through the train, weaving everyone all together. Gradually, the vision faded away and the profound feeling of loving connection as well.

Mark shared this experience with me in an email about ten days after it happened and asked if we could meet. "This was my first spiritual experience." he told me. "I tried to sustain that feeling of Oneness and great love and connection, and then became sad when I realized it was ending." I was quite surprised to hear his story, asking myself, "How could someone have such a deeply mystical experience of Union when not actively engaged or interested in spirituality, and on a New York subway of all places?"

When Mark arrived for our meeting, he looked strained. He told me that he was having trouble sleeping since his experience and was confused. He added that he didn't feel very "solid" anymore, and that sometimes it seemed as though his life activities and relationships had lost their purpose. "What happened to me and what does it all mean?" he asked.

I realized immediately that Mark was not yet prepared psychologically or spiritually to understand and integrate this state of Union into his consciousness and everyday life. A *state* of spiritual transcendence is brief and transient. By contrast, a *stage* is a sustained way of being, as a result of engaging in on-going psycho-spiritual work.

Because Mark had had such a strong experience, I believed there could be very difficult challenges for him ahead unless he became clear about what had happened. Since he was my student at the University, as opposed to a client with whom I had a therapeutic relationship, my attempts to help him were limited to a few discussions.

"I understand why you feel unmoored," I said to Mark. "At this time in your life, your personality and physical appearance is all about your individuality and, like most people, your ego self has been taught to seek a platform from which to display its uniqueness. However, your soul's truth is a different matter; it seeks connection, not separation. The sense of Union you experienced is not so much a loss of your individuality as it is an interplay of Self with God. It is an exchange process, rather than a loss of distinction, a sense of semi-permeability which does not obliterate your personality, but transcends it."

Mark had closed his eyes while I was speaking and now, he opened them and I saw they were glistening. We sat in silence for a few moments. He then asked me why he had been feeling so upset since his experience. "In many ways," he said, "it felt like a really sacred kind of thing that happened to me that day, but as much as I try to keep up my regular life and schedule, everything feels different now. It's like, I think, what's the point of anything, anymore? Why come to Columbia, why continue my job, why do I even care any more about my friends?"

"Mark," I said, "you have actually had a glimpse of the third stage on the Western Spiritual Path. It is called Union. This is a very spiritually developed stage and in a case like yours, can most definitely cause major emotional upheaval. Why? Because you experienced a very big opening of your heart, but it was premature in terms of your development."

Whenever a dramatic, potentially transformative event occurs in a person's life, such as a birth, death, falling in love or any other life-changing experience, there is a great deal of adjustment that needs to take place before the new inner state becomes accepted and ultimately feels comfortable. A powerful spiritual experience can be even more disruptive, because it is outside of consensus reality.

Mark not only had to come to terms with a shift in his interpretation of reality; he also had to accept his sudden, although brief, capacity to experience such a "huge love." His subway experience brought up feelings of losing control, of fear, and also of excitement and wonder. His sense of identity, his goals for the future, and all his personal insecurities that had been repressed in his shadow self were suddenly catapulted up into conscious awareness. Thus, there would be much inner work needed in order to incorporate the experience into his personality and life.

Such experiences can be ignored and their power will eventually fade. But if there is the desire to go into deeper, richer territory, then courage and commitment is needed. If a person is willing to really "show up" for the challenge, then it will be necessary to deal with one's shadow. As I shared in the story of Craig in the last chapter, Light that initially brings bliss will also bring up inner darkness. But all this is for the good—it is part of a process that the mystics called *purification*—which is for ultimate healing and spiritual growth.

The Spiritual Crisis

Psychiatrist Robert Assagioli (1888–1974), an early pioneer in the field of humanistic and transpersonal psychology, was the founder of the psycho-spiritual movement called "Psychosynthesis." He still has many followers today. In his seminal paper, "Self-Realization and Psychological Disturbances," he writes about the potential relationship between spiritual practices and psychological problems. For example, he posits how a person's ego may become inflated as a result of intense spiritual experiences:

> Instances of such confusion are not uncommon among people who become dazzled by contact with truths too great or energies too powerful for their mental faculties to grasp and their personality to assimilate.[23]

In such cases the individual is essentially having a "spiritual crisis." Consider, however, that in today's world, a spiritual crisis can happen not only because it is intensely powerful, but because there is no guiding structure to help a person figure out what is going on. As I said in Chapter One, the primary psychiatric interpretation is that the kinds of spiritual confusion that Assagioli describes come from a pathologic brain. However, recent research shows that when an individual's consciousness expands, it can cause physiological changes in the brain. These changes are very similar whether for a nun in prayer, for a Buddhist monk meditating, or for some persons who are said to be having a psychotic break.[24]

Mark's story is an example of how such crises can begin. Craig's story in Chapter One is another, in that his experience, while not by any means as dramatic or mystical as that of Eckhart

Tolle, seriously impacted his life because he was so unprepared psychologically or spiritually to deal with it.

As part of their extensive studies into different states of consciousness, Stanislav and Christina Grof coined the term *spiritual emergency,* similar to what many refer to as a spiritual crisis. They defined such inner upheavals as:

> ...crises when the process of growth and change becomes chaotic and overwhelming. Individuals experiencing such episodes may feel that their sense of identity is breaking down, that their values no longer hold true, and that the very ground beneath their personal realities is radically shifting. In many cases, new realms of mystical and spiritual experience enter their lives suddenly and dramatically, resulting in fear and confusion. They may feel tremendous anxiety, have difficulty coping with their daily lives, jobs, and relationships, and may even fear for their own safety.[25]

Over the years, I have worked with many spiritual seekers who went through a spiritual emergency. One of the most challenging aspects is when the person doubts it. And unfortunately, distrust of one's own spiritual experience is more common than not. In my own case, even though at times I might have felt insecure and vulnerable, most of the time I trusted that what was happening to me was meaningful and had a purpose.

Sally Clay, advocate and consultant for a group of ex-psychiatric patients (The Portland Coalition for the

Psychiatrically Labeled), has written about the important role
that spirituality played in her recovery. She spent two years hospitalized while diagnosed with schizophrenia. During her time
in the hospital, she had a powerful spiritual experience. The following are her words about her experiences:

> My recovery had nothing to do with talk ther-
> apy, the drugs, or the electroshock treatments
> that I received; more likely, it happened in spite
> of these things. . . . For me, becoming mentally ill
> was always a spiritual crisis, and finding a spiritual
> model of recovery was a question of life or death.
> Finally, I could admit openly that my experiences
> were, and always have been, a spiritual journey—
> not sick, shameful, or evil.[26]

Clay also writes: "I was cured instantly—healed if you
will—as a direct result of my spiritual experience."[27]

Many years later, Clay went back to the hospital to review
her case records, and found herself described as having "decom-
pensated with grandiose delusions with spiritual preoccupa-
tions." She complains, that "not a single aspect of my spiritual
experience at the hospital was recognized as legitimate; neither
the spiritual difficulties nor the healing that occurred at the
end."[28]

The lack of sensitivity to the spiritual dimensions of her
experience, says Clay, was detrimental to her recovery.

Our Culture's "Lazy Assumption"

Evelyn Underhill was strong in her concern about our "lazy assumption" that somehow science is real and spirituality is not. "We must pull down our own card houses," she said, "descend as the mystics say, into our nothingness, and examine for ourselves the foundations of all possible human experience, before we are in a position to criticize the buildings of the visionaries, the poets, the saints."[29]

The next chapter takes a brief look at why so many people today pay scant attention to visionaries of the past. It also offers a possible explanation for why our dominant societal beliefs and support systems play a part in creating the prevailing stress, confusion and angst in today's world.

CHAPTER 3

WORLDVIEWS AND SUPPORT SYSTEMS

We need a worldview grounded in science that does not deny the richness of human nature and the validity of modes of knowing other than scientific. If we can bring our spirituality, the richness and wholesomeness of our basic human values, to bear upon the course of science in human society, then the different approaches of science and spirituality will contribute together to the betterment of humanity.

—His Holiness, the Dali Lama (2012)

One of the great challenges of life is to say "yea" to that person or act or that condition which in your mind is the most abominable..

—Joseph Campbell and Bill Moyer,
The Power of Myth (1988)

Some years ago, I made a presentation at a large conference for psychologists and psychiatrists. My particular lecture emphasized the pervasive spiritual content found in the inner worlds of people with psychotic diagnoses, and suggested methods for helping them to understand and work with this religious material. Many participants who attended my talk were enthusiastic about this new perspective because, as therapists who worked with a mentally ill population, they realized that what I said was relevant for their clients. I felt good about their feedback and therefore was not prepared for what happened soon after.

A major keynote address followed, and I was one among approximately a thousand attendees in the audience, which consisted mostly of professionals who work with seriously mentally ill individuals. The speaker, whom I'll call "Dr. S.," was a psychiatrist of national prominence, and his talk focused on ways to work with psychotic patients. He initially spoke about the proper medication to use, and then continued with a discussion on why it is important to provide some sort of psychotherapy as well.

I was glad to hear Dr. S. say this, because I knew that for many psychotherapists, the primary treatment is medication and this often is a substitute for one-to-one psychotherapy. But then, a big knot in my stomach began to develop when I heard his next words: "Never, under any circumstances," he said, "engage in any conversation with patients about things which are not real. Stick to topics like holding a job, taking medication, carrying out activities of daily living, and practicing social skills."

When the time came for questions and answers, I raised my hand and asked him how he worked with patients in relation to their religious concerns, feelings, and fears, which I added, were prevalent with persons in psychotic states of consciousness. He stared right at me and impatiently replied, "As I said before, never, under any circumstances, engage in any conversation with patients about things that are not real."

I could not help myself and responded: "Am I correct that you are saying that spirituality is not real? We should therefore conclude that the religious beliefs that exist for the majority of people around the world, from time immemorial, are in fact, not real?"

There was a deafening silence that lasted for several moments. And then suddenly, Dr. S. turned on his heel, left the podium, and was gone. What to make of his reaction? I guess he might have been a little reluctant to answer, "Yes, most of the world is living in delusion." So, instead, he stormed out of the room. I slumped in my seat with burning cheeks and a pounding heartbeat as the master of ceremonies, a representative from the pharmaceutical firm supporting the conference, rushed to the stage, and asked the audience to thank Dr. S. for his outstanding presentation. He received a standing ovation for several minutes, even though he never returned to the stage.

As hundreds of people slowly filed out of the auditorium, I remained seated, feeling unsettled and the target of many curious, or even derisive, looks. There were a few individuals who walked toward me, however, and said things like, "Thanks for trying" and "What did you expect, you know how the system is." There was also a young woman who introduced herself to me as Jane, and who came over to shake my hand after the others had walked away. With her eyes full of tears, she told me that she would never forget my words. "I am a patient," she offered, "and I have never learned to tell the difference between the words of the good angels and the words of the bad ones inside my head. None of my therapists," she added, "will discuss this with me, and the medicine I am taking won't make the voices go away. I'm desperate."

I will come back to the question of inner voices in chapter six.

Our Three Dominant Worldviews

Deep down, we long to find a belief system that will never fail us, even in our darkest hour. It provides a structure for understanding ourselves, which affects our choices, values, levels of faith, and the way we live in the world. Such conclusions about what is true also become imprinted in human consciousness, and are transmitted from one time period to another. Thus, although a worldview is intimately related to a particular culture during a specific era and place, its influence can last for many hundreds of years, even when society has significantly changed.

Understandably, many people only feel secure if they maintain the same worldview as their community, friends, and relatives. When one's belief system begins to change, which can happen after a powerful spiritual experience, it can often feel traumatic. As we will see in the last section of this book, such feelings are a typical challenge in the first stage of spiritual development, especially in a culture that does not support the idea of such a path.

There are three dominant worldviews in our culture: the Premodern, Modern, and Postmodern. Each serves as a "super theory" or paradigm for interpreting human experience. Even though these arose during different historical time periods, our culture still remains deeply divided over which view is the right one.

- The Pre-modern view comes from the Middle ages, when the Church was the ultimate authority, governing every aspect of a person's life. An example today would be any extreme fundamentalist group. The leadership is totally in charge of what one should believe and how one should act. They hold the exclusive right to define, interpret, and teach about the soul and any spiritual belief system.

- The Modern view holds that nothing is true unless it can be verified by the scientific method;

- The Postmodern view holds that there is no absolute truth, because everything is relative and determined by individual perceptions.

When it comes to personal spiritual experiences, the Premodern rejects them, the Modern says they are a product of our biology and brain-based, and the Postmodern view maintains they have no objective validity or real meaning.

Our Support Systems Based on Our Worldviews

Each of these three worldviews has initiated a support system to help people when life is disrupted and beliefs are tested. In the Pre-modern view, there was the belief that humans had lost touch with the source, or had "fallen from God." Therefore, it became necessary for religion to devise its own rules, to mandate divine reward and punishment. Individuals would only receive "support" through following the dictates of the leadership.

This is relatively uncommon in contemporary Western culture. In today's mainstream religion, people have free will in terms of how they want to practice their faith. Unlike Pre-modernism, people are not condemned for heresy by the church. A wide variety of religious denominations from the liberal to the conservative each offer their own particular form of support.

The Modern view has given us our mental health support systems. The Postmodern view also provides supports, especially dominated by self-help and various New Age groups.

In and around these varying belief systems, we find some very difficult contradictions. What if a person's belief system fits into the Postmodern perspective, where the only thing considered real is subjective perception? Such a person might at the same time practice yoga, meditate and even believe in a Higher power. If the postmodern view is that the only reality is peoples' perceptions, then this creates a split in the core of one's being and spirituality can't exist. I say this because a belief in God means to believe in something that is Absolute, not something relative to one's perceptions. Even practicing yoga and meditating infers that there is a power, a source, an energy to which we are connected. This is, therefore, not a mere subjective belief.

Worldviews on Demand

Many people today are doing a mix-and-match of worldviews as might apply to their current life situation. Carol, for example, is a young attorney, primarily working as a social activist. Her story also points to big contradictions that can exist when a particular worldview that one holds is not consistent with one's sense of self, identity, and needs. Carol likes to think of herself as a postmodern agnostic who believes there is no such thing as good or bad, right or wrong. "It's just your mindset that makes things look one way or another," says Carol. "If something upsets you, just change your mind."

A staunch believer in holistic health, Carol subscribes to a New Age, mind/body perspective. Illness is a result of some unprocessed negative thought or feeling. Healing, therefore, will occur as a result of thinking and feeling differently.

This Postmodern view worked for her in the abstract until her father had a serious heart attack. During his weeks of recuperation, she shifted to a Modern perspective and spent many hours researching and meeting with medical experts who could provide scientific data explaining why her father had become ill, and which medications and medical procedures would ensure that he would recover. Her holistic health perspective no longer held up when she saw that her father's healing was not going to result from a change of his mind.

Thankfully, her father recovered, but let's assume for a moment that he did not. Where could Carol go for help with her grief and loss? Her Postmodern worldview would not sustain her; she would find that grief is not "relative," and possibly even life-shattering. Science could provide medication to blunt the pain, but would have little to offer in terms of helping her to process the deep impact of death on her identity and life-purpose.

Let's say that Carol experienced a vision of her deceased father standing by her bed and smiling at her, what then? Reports of after-death communication occur in a significant percentage of the population,[30] but our helping systems typically do not acknowledge the phenomenon. This means that many people are left without answers or support during a critical time in their lives.

In my experience, Carol is typical of large numbers of people who adhere to this same mix of worldviews in their lives. None of the described support systems that reflect these worldviews are completely right or wrong, but the problem is that they contradict one another. As a result, many people hold inner conflict and confusion over what they believe and who they are, and end up like the child raised by warring parents who never provide a stable and secure home.

In the following section, our different support institutions are described, with examples that show areas where they fail people struggling to find a stable belief system.

Religion, Our First Support System

Deirdre was an African-American student of mine who recently told me about her loss of faith at the age of nine. She grew up in a religious middle-class family and there was also a close relationship with extended family members. Life was bright and joyful until her father suddenly died. Her beloved grandfather died a week after that, followed by her sister Jody six months later. Although Deirdre was devastated by the losses, she was comforted by a vision she had one night, which told her that her beloved family members were together in heaven.

Several months later, Sister Martin, Deirdre's Catholic Sunday school teacher, asked the class to draw a picture of an angel. Deirdre drew not just one, but three. First, she drew a picture of her sister being carried up to heaven by her grandfather, who had angel wings. She drew her father, also with wings, waiting for them on a cloud. Then she took a crayon and carefully colored their skin a beautiful brown, just like hers.

When Sister Martin saw Deirdre's picture, she briskly informed her that there were no brown angels in Heaven. Not to be dissuaded, Deirdre passionately tried to talk about her vision of her grandfather's spirit returning for her sister.

"Nonsense!" snorted Sister Martin. She grabbed the picture and tore it up. And Deirdre was crushed. Here was an authority figure that had inspired her with stories about heaven, and now she was told that there was no place there for people like her. She was so devastated that she lost her resilience, her faith, and her identity. And when her family saw their little girl's anguish, they left the church and lost their moorings also. Deirdre vacillated between depression, anger, and acting out in the following years.

It is a tragedy that one individual could cause such trauma and devastation for one child and her family. Clearly, there are many sensitive, caring nuns who would be outraged at Sister Martin's behavior. This example is given to point to the damage that can be created in peoples' lives when important institutions fail them. Because Deirdre's family was deeply religious, the very first place they would look for support was in their church. And yet there was no help there for someone like Deirdre. Because of the nun's prejudice, Deirdre's mystical vision did not fit in with Sister Martin's belief system.

Deirdre's story is one example of how a support system that she trusted, and on which she had built her faith and sense of self, failed her when she needed it most. I have heard from many individuals who went to their priest, minister, or rabbi after having spiritual experiences that left them confused, only to be dismissed. Renée comes to mind, a successful forty-year-old computer programmer who went to see her minister after she began having dreams of dancing with a skeleton, which seemed to her to represent Death. Her unease was heightened when the minister told her to see a psychiatrist because he did not know how to help her.

Many people have turned away from their religious heritage for all sorts of reasons that have nothing to do with the sacred. For example, they reject it because of failures having to do with prejudice against women and revelations of sexual abuse. There is also the long history of violence exemplified by the religious crusades, torture, witch burnings, and totalitarian despots who killed in the name of Christ. While such concerns are understandable, it is important to know that direct spiritual experience has nothing to do with present or past institutional or human corruption.

It is also deeply disturbing to realize that we are living in a time when a war might erupt because of religious orthodoxy on a global scale. When these concerns are coupled with examples of responses from people like Sister Martin and Renée's minister, it is not surprising that Western religion is failing great numbers of people.

Our Second Support System: Psychology and Its Multiple Theories and Worldviews

There are many different psychological theories and approaches. What follows is a brief outline of what I believe to be the four main schools of psychology being practiced today. Each has based its therapeutic approach on a certain belief about human nature. This Psychology 101 approach is useful because I have found many people will choose a therapist without understanding the worldview and therapeutic approach that will govern their treatment. My aim, therefore, is to encourage people to take responsibility for their own health and well-being, especially while seeking support from professionals.

Psychoanalysis

Psychoanalysis evolved from the work of Sigmund Freud in the late 1800s and early 1900s. His influence on the fields of psychology, psychiatry and even education has been immense. One of his important contributions has been his work on the Unconscious, which has been validated both scientifically and clinically. Other significant contributions have been his emphasis on the relevance and quality of childhood experiences. This has an important effect on adult personality development, and the role of transference and free association in the therapy itself. Few people today consider the implications of his atheism, and therefore, the probable atheism of his followers. His view of human nature was generally pessimistic. He believed that it is the function of society to restrain people from acting out their innately dark and destructive instincts. But one cannot help but wonder where psychology would be today had Freud not rejected the Sacred. He said:

> Religion is an attempt to get control over the sensory world, in which we are placed, by means of the wish-world, which we have developed inside us as a result of biological and psychological necessities.[31]

Paradoxically, even though Freud did not believe in a Higher Power, there is a parallel between psychoanalysis and the Pre-modern view. He alleged that humans need to be supervised and controlled because they are inherently inclined towards negative and self-defeating behavior.

Behaviorism and Cognitive Behavioral Therapy (CBT)

Cognitive behavioral therapy (CBT), principally developed by psychologists Albert Ellis (1913–2007) and Aaron Beck (1921–) in the 1960s, began with the assumption that psychological distress is primarily the result of maladaptive patterns in the way people think.[32,33] Consequently, it has become a type of "rational" psychotherapy that attempts to alter behavior in order to change dysfunctional thoughts and emotions. It is used for treating such conditions as anger, depression, anxiety, eating disorders, addictions, and phobias. A typical intervention might be designed to create an aversion toward something in order to alter the behavior, such as associating cigarette smoke with an unpleasant odor. It is a multilevel approach for investigating the mechanics of how people learn and respond to stimuli and reinforcements.[34]

CBT psychology is most easily aligned with the Modern worldview. In many ways, practitioners see themselves as social engineers. The human being is regarded as a complex type of machine or animal, responsive to testing and training and sometimes even manipulation. More recently, Martin Seligman took CBT in a more optimistic direction and started a movement that has come to be known as "positive psychology." It proposes that people can shift dysfunctional worldviews and self-beliefs to those that are more constructive, by deciding to think positively.[35] While the advantages of more optimistic thinking can certainly hold appeal for many, it is my belief that positive psychology views the human spirit in a superficial way. It solely values cognition at the expense of emotions, the shadow and the soul.

Humanistic psychology

The predecessor of positive psychology was introduced in 1962 by psychologist Abraham Maslow, with his book *Toward a Psychology of Being,* in which he described a "humanistic psychology."[36] Maslow's work came out of a collaboration in the late 1950s with psychologists Carl Rogers (1902–1987), and Rollo May (1909–1994), whose concern was for a happier, more optimistic psychology than either psychoanalysis or behaviorism. The fundamental view is that people are born whole and innately good; thus, the approach focuses on issues such as self-actualization, love, creativity, and individuality.

Humanistic psychology is a step in the right direction, but at the same time, there is minimal acknowledgement of the soul. Instead, it teams up with the postmodern worldview, stressing that individual feelings and perceptions are the whole story. This leaves the person's ego in the center of his or her own universe, eliminating anything existing beyond the small self. Psychiatrist Fritz Perls (1893–1970), originator of Gestalt therapy, created the "Gestalt prayer," which summarizes the essential view: "I do my thing, you do your thing, and if we find each other, it's beautiful."[37]

Although during the Sixties and Seventies people found Perls' work very liberating, its effect has left many with the belief that life has no intrinsic meaning.

I'll talk about the "fourth school," which is transpersonal psychology and the New Age movement, in a moment. But first we need to look at two problems mainstream psychology has with spirituality.

Why Psychology Avoids Spirituality

Despite the growing influence of a more positive psychology,[38] the view that the human being is merely some sort of animal or machine still wields an enormous amount of power, both in our culture and in professional and academic psychology. The first reason has to do with the fear of mental illness; the second with the considerable power and influence of the field of biochemistry.

The First Reason: "Fear of "Going Crazy"

Since there can be a fine line between heightened states of consciousness and what is interpreted as psychosis, it is a powerful fear not only for the public, but for mental health professionals as well. The words of the highly regarded psychiatrist Dr. S., who said, "Never talk about things that are not real," could be a bumper sticker for the current state of much of the profession. The worry is that somehow engaging in discussions about a person's strong spiritual energies will take the helping professional into areas that cannot be controlled. It becomes easier and psychologically less stressful to prescribe higher doses of medication. This brings us to biochemistry, the tidy solution for attempting to numb not only emotional pain, but personal spiritual experience as well.

The Second Reason: "Building a Better Brain Through Chemistry"

Over the last few decades, psychotherapy has increasingly shifted from talk therapy to the use of pharmaceuticals to manage and suppress symptoms of psychic suffering. The shift began in the 1990s, which the National Institute of Mental Health (NIMH) called the "Decade of the Brain."[39] Today, millions of children and adults have been led to believe that the primary source of a psychological ailment is a neurological mishap. In the last few years, for example, a "pacemaker for the brain" was introduced to treat depression. This device is surgically implanted in the chest to activate parts of the brain when a client has not responded to psychotherapy or drugs.[40]

Often psychiatrists work in tandem with psychologists to offer both cognitive behavioral modification and drugs. While both psychotropic medication and cognitive behavioral psychotherapy may lessen symptoms for a time, unaddressed emotional wounds and spiritual yearnings invariably persist, resulting in clients becoming more despondent and the psychological establishment feeling more helpless. In my view, the devotion of the field of mental health to this current model can at times be extremely damaging, as the following example shows:

Janine and the Incurable Brain

Recently while on a vacation, I called a plumber to help with an issue in our kitchen and we got to chatting. His name was Paul and when he learned I was a psychologist, he asked me shyly, and with an undertone of desperation, if I would mind talking with his wife Janine. "She has seen lots of different doctors and no one can help her," he said. "I don't know what to do."

Janine turned out to be an attractive woman in her late thirties, very thin and with dark shadows under her eyes. When we sat down together, she shared a bit about certain strange "feelings" she had that were causing her anxiety, stress and confusion. Then she pulled out a sketch that her most recent psychiatrist had made to help explain her "condition." I asked about her diagnosis and was told that she had been labeled psychotic and had been hospitalized at one point.

The drawing by Janine's psychiatrist depicted three kinds of brains. The "normal" one was basically clear inside, the second one was a mixture of clear and some black squiggles, and the third one, the abnormal brain, was all black inside. He had told her that she had the misfortune to have the third kind of brain and her problem therefore was incurable. And he had thus far prescribed 20 different kinds of medications to experiment with managing her symptoms. They made her feel terrible and even more stressed, so she had stopped taking them.

Privately I was shocked and angry. How could a mental health professional treat a client so callously? How could he be so irresponsible in terms of the approach he was taking with her medication?

I asked Janine if she had any kind of spiritual faith. Both she and Paul explained that they had attended church when young, but now were "spiritual but not religious." "Is there anything spiritual that you do to help yourself when you are stressed?" I asked.

Janine became a bit embarrassed, but finally said that the only time she became calm was when "Dog" came to her. Paul gave a start and raised his eyebrows in surprise, since Janine had never spoken of it before. We continued to talk and the more Janine shared, the more she was able to relax. She had had numerous spiritual experiences, including visions of Jesus, but she felt they were so unacceptable in the context of no longer being "religious," that she had to give "Him" a hidden name.

Thus, her source of strength was "Dog."

The idea that spiritual experience and psychological and emotional pain are merely chemical disruptions in the brain has three negative outcomes:

1. The complexities of human nature, spiritual experience, and the soul are denied;

2. Drug therapy often causes unpleasant and sometimes dangerous physiological side effects;

3. When people learn from experts that they need to depend on chemicals to function, they learn to see themselves as permanently damaged victims instead of basically strong and competent.

When psychiatry and psychology place too much emphasis on the mechanics of brain chemistry, practitioners no longer meet their clients on a human level, let alone at the level of soul. For clients, the authority of the doctor can be so powerful and intimidating that they either completely give up their own deepest spiritual longings, or try to secretly hold onto them, with little success. A case in point: Marta is a social worker with a deep interest in spirituality. She has an altar in her bedroom, keeps a journal of her dreams, goes on vision quests, and talks about spiritual matters with her clients. At the same time, she has spent more than a decade going to a psychiatrist who does not believe that she has a soul and who tells her that she will never be able to function in life without medication for her frequent episodes of depression. Clearly, she is deeply conflicted about her belief system and very dependent on her psychiatrist. And even though she is a mental health professional herself, she does not trust her own faith and spiritual process. Her depression is testimony to this sad stalemate in her life.

With such influences from the medical model, it is not surprising that a large part of the population is becoming drug-addicted. How could it be otherwise? Yet, there is hope. Some psychiatric professionals are publishing books that challenge the excessive focus on pharmacology and psychiatric drugs in the field.[41] Consumer advocacy groups (including activists like Sally Clay) who rebel and make a public argument against their treatment, are increasing in numbers.

Transpersonal Psychology and the New Age Movement

When Carl Jung broke off his relationship with his mentor Sigmund Freud, the field of psychology was at a crossroads. Jung's *depth psychology* advocated a personal relationship with the Sacred as necessary for mental health. Thus, he is one of the early heroes of transpersonal psychology, which has tried to create a vision of a psychologically-informed spirituality and a spiritually-based psychology. The term transpersonal means beyond the personal and its core assumption is that the individual is a spiritual being as well as a self-conscious organism or psychological ego.[42]

While highly motivated to right existing wrongs, transpersonal psychology is still in its infancy. Since it is the only approach today in the discipline of psychology to focus on consciousness and the spiritual realm, there are many questions that must be answered as it matures:

- How much emphasis should it place on science and research?

- What spiritual traditions should be emphasized, if any?

- How do transpersonal psychologists relate to their more mainstream colleagues, who tend to marginalize their spiritual orientation, regularly lumping them together with the New Age movement?

- How do they come to terms with their own personal (positive and negative) childhood religious memories and experiences?

- Which worldview do they hold, and how does it impact their work with their clients?

Challenges abound.

The Diagnostic Category "Religious or Spiritual Problem"

In 1994, it appeared as if a major step forward in psychology took place when a new diagnostic category entitled "Religious or Spiritual Problem" was included in the fourth edition of the *Diagnostic and Statistical Manual of Mental Disorders* (DSM-IV). This book, now in its fifth edition, is considered by some as the "bible" for the fields of psychiatry and psychology in terms of diagnosis and treatment of various forms of mental illness.

The category "Religious or Spiritual Problem" is authored by four clinicians and researchers from the Department of Psychiatry at the University of California in San Francisco.[43]

One of these is David Lukoff, Ph.D., who himself had a dramatic spiritual crisis as a young adult.[44] Even though this category was listed as a "V code," a collection of diagnoses buried in the back section of the manual, the hope was that it would help create a new relationship between psychiatry, religion, and spirituality. It was designed to benefit both mental health professionals and those who seek their assistance.

The category identifies a *religious problem* as a person's conflicting feelings about the beliefs, practices, rituals, and experiences related to a religious institution. This is to distinguish it from a *spiritual problem,* defined as distress associated with a person's relationship to a Higher Power or transcendent force that is unrelated to a religious organization.

Clinicians in the transpersonal field at the time believed that this new category in the DSM–IV was a great breakthrough. For the first time, there was the acknowledgment that distressing religious and spiritual experiences were non-pathological issues.

I also had hoped it would correct the many misdiagnoses and mistreatment of persons in the midst of spiritual emergencies. Now, years later, I am disappointed to say that spiritual emergencies are not generally acknowledged as such by the great majority of mental health professionals. There have been numerous times when I would try to inform a psychiatrist about this category, only to be the recipient of a blank and annoyed stare.

The New Age Movement and the
Spiritual-But-Not-Religious

For nearly a half-century, many people in the West have left both Judaism and Christianity in order to study and practice such spiritual traditions as Hinduism, Buddhism, Sufism, Wicca, and Shamanism, largely because they each include some type of meditative practice or way to alter consciousness. Such questing came in part because of the rejection of Western organized religion and also because of the modern worldview that states we are merely physical bodies and mechanical brains. It also is a result of increasing commitment to a multi-cultural global unity. An entire sub-culture centered on self-knowledge and self-help has fostered an industry serving millions.

As positive as the desire for self-knowledge and worldwide communication may seem, frequently people discover that the inner world is not always easy to understand and navigate alone. Discovering and strengthening one's identity is necessary for any form of human development, and guidance is often needed. A spiritual counselor can be very helpful at such a time. However, it can be difficult and sometimes even harmful when counselors do not have any in-depth understanding or training in either psychology or in psycho-spiritual work. As I've said, there are few agreed-upon standards in the New Age movement. When clients open up to very powerful spiritual energies, unresolved emotional issues that have been suppressed frequently are pushed to the surface. If there is no qualified spiritual teacher, psychotherapist, or guide present, a spiritual crisis may manifest.

There are two more reasons why New Age spirituality often fails to provide the kind of guidance so badly needed today:

Reason 1: Discounting the Influence of our Western Mystical Roots

Even though transpersonal psychology acknowledges the universal and cross-cultural commonalities in all spiritual traditions, many healers and spiritual counselors primarily give credence to Eastern or indigenous, shamanistic spiritual traditions and practices. This results in a disconnection with our Western spiritual heritage.

Chapter five will look more closely at why people, whose roots and identity come from Western civilization and the Judeo-Christian tradition, need to be aware of its influence. For now, I will simply point out that the New Age movement tends to bypass this issue in large part because it is full of people who have rejected organized religion. In addition, there is the widespread belief, which is incorrect, that expanded states of spiritual consciousness, typically accessed through the practice of meditation, are not part of our Western spiritual tradition.

For example, many spiritual counselors will support a seeker with a "kundalini awakening" (the Hindu name connected with a spiritual opening—usually the result of a powerful energy surge in the body). The energy of "the Holy Spirit," however, is almost never mentioned. In spite of the fact that topics such as good and evil, light and darkness, or Jesus and Satan, come through the consciousness of many Western seekers on the spiritual path, many New Age therapists become uneasy when such themes come up. As stated previously, they will often refer a client with such concerns to a psychiatrist, who then may very well prescribe medication.

Reason 2: Avoiding the Shadow

New Age practices are often about exploring stored energy in the body, past lives, shamanic journeying, near-death-experiences, and a myriad of other related topics. More often than not, however, many avoid addressing "the shadow"—those uncomfortable parts of ourselves that Jung said are repressed, such as fear, anger, jealousy, and greed. When spiritual seekers access these challenging emotions, they need considerable assistance to face, work with, and integrate the strong energies that arise. Yet the primary focus is more often on the light within, while fears, shadow, and unresolved emotional angst that invariably get pushed up with heightened consciousness are bypassed.

Debi's story is a good example of this problem:

Jesus is Not PC

Debi attended a weeklong workshop for guided meditation led by the well-known transpersonal therapist "Dr. T." After each session, participants were invited to share their meditation experiences. When it came Debi's turn, she described a powerful vision she had had of Jesus. A deafening silence followed. Debi later told me, "There seemed to be a mix of reactions: discomfort from those who had rejected Christianity (many were followers of Buddhism); awe from some, and perhaps resentment or even envy from others as well." No one gave her any feedback, including Dr. T., so she began to feel isolated from the group and nervous whenever it was her turn to speak. Several days after Debi's sharing, Dr. T., in a neutral manner, said something about how both Buddha and Jesus were enlightened beings. By that time Debi was feeling somewhat insecure since she had had such a "politically incorrect" vision. In Debi's next meditation, a fragment of a memory about childhood sexual abuse appeared. When she shared her concerns with the group, several people thanked her for opening up the space for more serious material. Yet one member had made it clear early in the workshop that he was just there to have an "enlightened" time, so he was not happy with her "depressing" revelations. Dr. T., however, invited Debi to meditate further in order to delve more deeply into the memory.

Debi followed his suggestion and had several breakthrough insights about her grandfather's abuse, her buried rage, her issues with her parents, and how these were all inextricably connected. Dr. T. then invited her to share, but when a lot of emotion came along with the sharing, he impatiently cut her off with, "Well, we don't have much time, please get to the conclusion."

Debi was crushed. "It took me right to that feeling I always had as a child, of being so disempowered that I could not even try to express how things were for me," she said. "If I could have felt heard and accepted, I might have begun the process of healing and would have been able to attend to the meditations as the workshop continued. But it was clear that people were unnerved by my process. No one said anything like, 'I've been there too, you'll get through it,' or, 'If you'd like to talk more, I'd be happy to listen.'"

From that time forward, Debi's isolation increased. "Once people had decided I was unevolved," she explained, "there wasn't really anything I could do to change their view." Debi described how even Dr. T. seemed unable to allow her to relax and be herself. There was a lot of levity at the workshop, but when he spoke to Debi, he would become more serious, as if he felt he had to walk on eggshells with her.

Several members of the group did approach her to offer tips on self-help books, workshops, and other ways that Debi could get more assistance. One woman optimistically suggested that she get more exercise. What no one seemed to grasp was that receiving memories and insights were not the problem. Debi had been blocking her issues for years, and the meditation had brought them forth with great intensity. And she was grateful: "It was a wonderful gift and a blessing to have access to the feelings and information that came up. It just wasn't pretty."

Shortly after arriving home, Debi wrote in her journal: "I'm not who I was. I don't know where I'm going. I hate myself." I began to work with Debi after this crushing experience. I supported her new and fragile relationship with Jesus as her inner spiritual guide. As her connection with her inner light strengthened, memories of the abuse, which now, it became clear, was from her grandfather, also began to surface. After some months passed, Debi and I met with her parents and she was able to talk about what had happened to her. Her mother affirmed her memories and finally, Debi was able to heal and come home to herself.

Having discussed key issues that I believe are causing much angst in our culture, the next section presents my thoughts about what is missing. So I'll begin by talking about God.

PART TWO

OUR WESTERN
SPIRITUAL ROOTS

CHAPTER 4

GOD EXPERIENCE

*God is an infinite sphere, whose center is everywhere
and circumference is nowhere.*

—Turba Philosophorum, early medieval times

*I had an experience I can't prove. I can't even explain
it, but everything I know as a human being, everything that I am tells me that it was real. I was part
of something wonderful, something that changed me
forever, a vision of the Universe that tells us undeni-
ably how tiny and insignificant, and how rare and
precious we all are. A vision that tells us we belong
to something greater than ourselves. That we are not,
that none of us is alone.*

—Carl Sagan, (1997)

According to a 2011 Gallup poll, nine out of ten Americans say
they believe in God.[45] On one end of the spectrum, we have conservative believers who hope to restore traditional family values
and follow their interpretations of the Bible. This group includes

orthodox Jews who practice the same Jewish traditions and follow the scriptures in the Old Testament (the Torah) as Jews have done for thousands of years. It also includes born-again Christians, who live according to literal interpretations of the New Testament.

On the other end, we have a broad assortment of increasingly liberal churches and synagogues, where social and political activism is a major focus and the concept of God is often secondary to a debate over its definition. Meanwhile, the "spiritual but not religious" won't go near the term, but have shifted to references like "Higher Power." The tension between conservative versus liberal religious beliefs has become deeply divisive in Western culture, with many people eager to avoid identification with one extreme or the other. I have a colleague at Columbia University who has a strong faith, but hides a cross under her blouse for fear that the symbol will be misinterpreted as right-wing ideology.

When I raise the subject of God in my course on spiritual development, inevitably, one or more of my students will flare up. Josh is a typical example. He was immediately upset and quick to announce that he does not believe in "the Big Guy in the Sky." I ask other members of the class if they agree. There is a passionate discussion. I'm working with psychology graduate students with predominantly a postmodern view, so I often hear: "God can't be proved scientifically;" "It's just a superstition;" or, "People want to believe because they are afraid of the challenges of life and fear death." But then, there is always someone like Caroline. She quietly shares that God brings her peace and happiness. She is certain He brought her to Columbia to fulfill her dream of helping people.

Josh becomes frustrated and red in the face as he tries to explain himself. I cool things down by asking him about his inner life, whether, for example, he has had any precognitive experiences, significant dreams, or transcendent feelings in nature. He is reluctant and embarrassed at first, but finally shares an experience he had where his grandfather came to him after the man's death.

"And what did that mean to you?" I ask.

"I don't know," he shrugs. I ask the class whether anyone else has had an experience with a departed loved one. A number of students share, some with emotion and even tears. After class, Josh comes up to me and says that he feels very confused. We talk, and I think afterwards that it often seems the more passionate the naysayer, the deeper the inner conflict. Someone like Josh is usually longing for unshakeable truth, but it's not surprising that he doesn't know where to begin to look.

Carl Jung was asked near the end of his life whether he believed. He answered, "I don't believe. I know." Josh is having trouble getting there because of the influences of today's scientific and postmodern world.

God, an Experience of Divine Love

In my life and work, I use the word God because of my desire to reclaim its original meaning, its mystical truth, at the core of our Judeo-Christian heritage. That is to say, not as a concept, but as an experience. The many definitions of the indefinable bear only a partial relationship to the feelings of awe, wisdom, wonder, inspiration, joy, and love that have been documented across the ages, from mystics to ordinary men, women, and children. Without words, it is easier to come close to what God is for us mortals. Artists, poets, and musicians do the best job; they show rather than tell. And writers do best with story. Like this one I share about Emily, 35 years old, a happily married agnostic accountant, mother of two, with many close friends and family ties. A perfect life but for one dark spot: her estrangement from her brother Michael, a result of his many cruel remarks and dismissive behavior.

One night in a dream state, Emily became aware of an all-but-overwhelming love entering her entire being. There was ecstatic joy, a piercing sweetness, and then, a sense of profound peace and serenity. It may have lasted for seconds or for hours. She was unsure.

Despite her agnosticism, Emily instantly sensed it was an experience of God. Then there was an abrupt shift. Her brother appeared in the dream and she was filled with anger and sadness. But not for long. Again, the experience of love took over and she felt its power dissolve her pain until there was nothing left. In that same moment, she understood her brother's suffering and realized that his cruelty came from jealousy, a lack of self-esteem, and emotional wounds from childhood.

Emily awoke and was astonished to discover that her anger had been completely replaced by compassion and forgiveness. Since she had no religious background, she found this event amazing and inexplicable. She later told me that she had never known such a love, so deep and potent, it had completely filled every cell of her body and every corner of her mind and heart. "My heart felt expanded, open, and at peace," she said. "It was the greatest experience of my life."

I often witness such transformations after a person has a God experience. Emily could have dismissed the message in her dream, but she felt so liberated from pain, she could not sustain her former way of being.

Such experiences go beyond definitions and belief systems and scientific proof. It was a mystical experience, a pure, wordless, awareness of the Divine. First, comes the power of experience; then the understanding. Through Emily's story we can see how the mystical experience is pure, with the "center everywhere and circumference nowhere," before and beyond the formation of a concept.

The 16th century nun Teresa of Avila, later canonized by the Catholic church, wrote: "It is a caressing of love so sweet which now takes place between the soul and God, that I pray God of His goodness to make him experience it who may think that I am lying."[46]

Most people can accept that love is a vital exchange of energy in relationship with another. There is nothing abstract about love. And there is nothing abstract about God. Without knowing God as a living experience, all we have left is an empty construct. As such, it can have little transformative power or influence in our lives. Yet, as Emily's dream shows, the power of the God experience can happen to anyone, can change a life forever, and a person does not even need to be religious to have such an experience.

In *The Cloud of Unknowing,* an anonymous 14th century work of a Christian mystic, there is this:

> Our intense need to understand will always be a powerful stumbling block to attempts to reach God in simple love. . . and must always be overcome. For if you do not overcome this need to understand, it will undermine your quest. It will replace the darkness which you have pierced to reach God with clear images of something which, however good, however beautiful, however Godlike, is not God.[47]

Contrast those words with the increasing number of studies of journalists and professors who are envisioning possible applications for creating God experiences with medication,[48] analyzing whether oxytocin is a factor in spiritual experience, and whether brain synapses light up with spiritual openness[49] or whether evangelicals who have experiences of God are simply doing a sort of self-brainwashing.[50] The problem is that too many researchers seem to be stuck in the belief that evidence of brain changes during expanded states of consciousness is the whole story. Yes, there is evidence of change, but there is no explanation for why it occurs. To this I might add that not only is it not an adequate explanation, but it will not help the person who has had the experience know what to do next.

Back to the 14th century mystic who wrote in *The Cloud of Unknowing:* "When it comes to the subject of God," says the writer, "let go of the constructions you've built on your rational island. Become innocent. Jump into the water."[51]

The Three Faces of God

Ken Wilber, an American writer, internationally-recognized scholar on consciousness studies, and a long-term Buddhist, has in recent years begun looking more closely at Western spirituality. He suggests that at the fullest level of development, a person should be able to experience God in three ways, God as "I," the Self; God as the "All" ; and God as "Other," in an I/Thou relationship.[52]

God as I, the God Self

The following is an example of the experience of the "God self." This is the I AM, our inner wisdom, the God Within:

One night, 19-year-old Joe, a college freshman from a secular upper-middle-class Jewish family, sat alone in his college dorm room and suddenly had the breathtaking realization that he and God were one and the same. He knew this, not with his mind but with his entire being. He also understood that living consciously in the present moment would be essential from that point on. It would be the only way to sustain this enormous understanding.

Believing he had been given the key to the mystery of life, Joe became like a spiritual sage for a time. But he did not know what to do with what he had learned and eventually the power of the experience faded. He returned to his everyday life, but never forgot what he had seen and felt. He began coming to see me when he was in his late thirties, struggling with depression and a failing marriage, wondering why he could not recover the ecstasy and depth of that important time in his life.

"But Joe," I said, "You are creating an artificial split between your everyday life and the memory of what happened way back when, as though they cannot be one and the same. If you had a living experience of God before, why not consider you can feel it now as well?"

As we continued to talk over the weeks, Joe seemed to become more confused, lost and dependent on me, asking that I resolve his life situation. In order to bring him back to himself, I reminded him about something he had shared with me during an earlier session. He had told me that the experience of God that he encountered years before had been so intense and mind-blowing that he had to find a way to ground himself. He discovered that he could relieve panic and disorientation by sitting down with a paper and pen, focusing within and silently asking questions. By reaching deep in his soul, he could feel that original God connection come alive in him again. Quickly, without consideration, he would then write out the answers that came to him and they always provided guidance.

I gave Joe some paper and urged him to try his practice again. He wrote for two solid hours. By the end, he had become a different person—such wisdom and clarity had emerged! I was moved to tears when I read his writing. There were pages and pages of deep insight.

"Your therapist has become expendable," I told him.

God Self is also called God Immanent. It is our connection with Divine Intelligence, our soul's truth. When we tap into the flow of God energy within, we discover an ever-present support. When I asked Joe why he had not been doing his practice all along, he replied that he had lost faith and needed encouragement.

"I don't believe that you are afraid to trust that God is within you," I said. "It's because you are afraid of what that guidance will be."

Joe knew intellectually, for example, that he needed to end the pattern of unhealthy dependency and repressed anger in his marriage. He also knew that he needed to spend time alone and become stronger in himself. But his personality, fears and attachments kept getting in the way and he did not feel able to take action. Yet when he accessed his soul's truth, he discovered a place of purity and strength, free of his ego and fears. When he connected with that Source, where there was healing and wisdom, he sat up straighter, spoke with conviction and looked more relaxed than I had seen him in months. He eventually left his unfulfilling job and began to have deep discussions with his wife, having gained the courage to tackle his biggest challenges. He could not have found this certainty through regular psychotherapy, however, because his problems did not rest in the realm of logic or emotions. The real issue was his difficulty in connecting with his soul and getting himself out of the way so that he could trust God.

While feeling connected to one's God Self can be a source of great strength and wellbeing, it can also be a common trap for people on the spiritual path, who cannot distinguish when their ego is doing the talking and when there is true wisdom coming through. Joe could have, for example, just written out a lot of personal wants and needs, as opposed to being open to divine wisdom. How do you tell the difference? Joe had previously experienced an authentic connection with God, and this made it easier for him to reconnect with his divine nature. This is an essential part of the spiritual path; it is why I encourage my clients to engage in a process such as Breathwork that helps them connect with their soul and expand their consciousness.

God as the All, as Oneness

God as the All can be understood as Oneness, the experience of becoming merged with everything—no inner, no outer, simple, "All." In her book *Reason for Hope: A Spiritual Journey*, renowned primatologist Jane Goodall describes a powerful experience she had during a time spent in the jungle:

> "Lost in the awe at the beauty around me, I must have slipped into a state of heightened awareness. It is hard—impossible, really—to put into words the moment of truth that suddenly came upon me then. Even the mystics are unable to describe their brief flashes of spiritual ecstasy. It seemed to me, as I struggled afterward to recall the experience, that self was utterly absent: I and the chimpanzees, the earth and trees and air, seemed to merge, to become one with the spirit power of life itself. The air was filled with a feathered symphony, the evensong of birds.

I heard new frequencies in their music and also in the singing insects' voices—notes so high and sweet I was amazed. Never had I been so intensely aware of the shape, the color of the individual leaves, the varied patterns of the veins that made each one unique. Scents were clear as well, easily identifiable: fermenting, overripe fruit; waterlogged earth; cold, wet bark; the damp odor of chimpanzee hair, and yes, my own too. And the aromatic scent of young, crushed leaves was almost overpowering."[53]

God as the All is a holistic perception of the great web of life—the perfection of Oneness, stretching from dust to Deity. I believe that Jane Goodall describes an experience of God in this latter aspect. Many great spiritual leaders and teachers throughout history can point to such events that were influential and guided their life's work. Here is another version, described by the American philosopher David Spangler:

"When I was seven years old . . . the domain of consciousness itself broke through and I had a classical mystical experience of dissolving into an oceanic feeling of oneness and infinite connectedness. I became pure consciousness, which was limitless and, if I were to give it a quality, infinitely loving. It was a beingness of love."[54]

Many seekers today are especially drawn to a definition of God-as-All, or God-as-Gaia. And while this is an important way to experience God, it is but one of three aspects. As with the "God Self," it is possible for one to have moments of transcendence and yet still keep the ego intact. But how to get rid of the sense of the separate self? How to surrender to an Absolute force, a higher consciousness that is available to help direct and guide one's life? This brings us to the biggest obstacle that many seekers have with the Western God: the anthropomorphic definition of a Father in the Sky.

God as Other, as "Thou"

Is there a "Who," a "Being" up there who is calling the shots?

Carl Jung wrote, "The unrelated human being lacks wholeness, for he can achieve wholeness only through the soul, and the soul cannot exist without its other side, which is always found in a You." [55] In other words, we each perceive ourselves as an "I", but we also perceive that we are not the whole story. That which completes us is only found in relationship.

The idea of God as Other, beyond the separate self, is a sticking point for many in the West and too reminiscent of the authority of organized religion. Yet Ken Wilber now says he has finally come to realize that "a relationship with that Other in love and devotion and ecstasy . . . is the only appropriate response if you have any sanity at all." [56] "Without God as Thou . . . becoming a living, felt dimension of our own direct experience of Spirit," he says, "I wonder whether it's possible to ever move beyond ego in any kind of authentic way." [57]

The personal relationship with God is well known in popular culture. There are books—both serious and humorous—about "talking with God," "having a conversation with God," and "how to pray to God," for example. Most of these are oriented towards the religious and cultural definition of God as Father in Heaven. The experience of God as Other, as Presence, is direct, and not that literal or filtered. Emily's dream, just described, is an example. She experienced the sensation of an external force, a flow and power of transcendent Love, infusing her entire self, transforming and healing her relationship with her brother.

Another example:

Paul was a commercial artist. His wife, Jane, was an elementary school teacher. Both were agnostic. They came to me to discuss an overwhelming experience Paul had had a few nights earlier. He was sitting and relaxing in the tub at home when suddenly, in an inexplicable instant, his sense of boundaries disappeared and he was enveloped in a powerful brilliant light. He felt the presence of God and heard what seemed like God's voice revealing profound wisdom about human nature, life and death. Time stood still. Several hours seemed to go by in a second.

In a heightened state of consciousness, Paul became aware of an infinite, all-seeing, all-knowing Presence, a divine force immeasurably greater than himself. He felt that his identity had been annihilated. After the experience eventually faded, he was deeply shaken, wondering whether he was going crazy.

Direct God energy such as Paul experienced is more than most of us can handle, which is why the role of the shaman or guru or some sort of spiritual guide has throughout the ages had an important function. The spiritual terrain is not easily navigated without support, especially in the beginning of the journey. In *The Tibetan Book of Living and Dying*, Tibetan Buddhist teacher Sogyal Rinpoche writes, "It is difficult to relate to the presence of enlightened energies if they have no form or ground for personal communication . . . personifying them in the form of deities enables the practitioner to recognize them and relate to them."[58] Rinpoche also notes, "they are a universal and fundamental experience, but the way they are perceived depends on our conditioning."[59]

In the West, our capacity to sense God as Other has resulted in the religious iconography of our Judeo-Christian heritage. This is also how I understand Jesus. He is the divine protector, teacher, and spiritual guide in the West. The Hindu gods and the Buddha, for example, fulfill this role in the East. Yet as Rinpoche says, "In whatever form the deities appear, it is important to recognize that there is definitely *no difference whatever in their fundamental nature* (my emphasis)."[60] In other words, they all point to the same Source, for every human, in every culture, around the world.

I once had a student named Rebecca, a woman who was working towards a Ph.D. in Jewish religious studies. She came to see me because, despite all of her years of study and commitment, she said she felt as if something was missing from her spiritual life. As we talked, she broke down and began to sob. She finally confessed that she was afraid to pray because ten years earlier, she had a spiritual experience of such intense love (which she knew was God) that she became overwhelmed. She feared she would be shattered by the power of this love, and immediately distanced herself from prayer. Through our discussions, she came to realize that her fear, and also her ego, were keeping her from her greatest spiritual yearning, to feel at one with God. Again, it is important for Western seekers to remember: the ego can survive intact with God as I AM and with God as All. But in relationship with the God as Other, there is no option but to surrender and give up control to this immensity, which is so much more powerful than our separate, individual self.

The call from the self to God-as-Other is fundamentally a question: "Do I deserve to be here?" It is a cry for confirmation, for unconditional, all-embracing, non-judgmental love and acceptance: Does my life matter? Do I, with all of my mistakes and confusions and baggage, still matter?

The God-as-Other experience shows that we do matter, and that we are not alone. Each of us is part of a Greater Whole, like an individual cell in one Body. At the same time, we are singular and with our own path and destiny.

Just as a musician longs to become the music, so that there is no barrier between the player and the song, the goal of spiritual development is ultimately to merge with God, to experience God in all three ways: within, throughout, and outside. And to become—freely, purely, the expression of the whole.

Aligning with God

Throughout history, one can find an infinite number of descriptions of miraculous events, lives saved, dangers averted, and dreams fulfilled. They are all considered evidence of the mysterious workings of God energy. When I talk about trusting and receiving guidance, it's important to understand that I'm not talking about a God figure who is controlling our lives. It is more accurate to say that when we are in alignment with God energy, experiences of heightened awareness reveal which choices will fulfill our life purpose. In Taoism, the idea is to "stay in the flow" in order to have life blossom naturally before you.

In the 1920s, Carl Jung and physicist Wolfgang Pauli took this concept very seriously. That is why, together, they coined the term *synchronicity*. They described synchronicity as an event that reveals a perfect match between inner experience and external reality, for example, thinking about a friend a nanosecond before she calls on the phone.

A particular synchronicity that was both inexplicable and profound for me still stands out in my mind. It took place when I was working as a consultant at Matrix Research Institute and involved in the Breathwork training program. Several times each year, I would take two weeks off, expand my consciousness in Breathwork, and enter into a completely different reality. Needless to say, my more conventionally-oriented Matrix colleagues had a challenging time figuring me out. Fortunately, Irv Rutman, a nationally recognized psychologist and the director of Matrix, supported my spiritual seeking even though he realized that there was no real interest in such a non-traditional perspective in the psychiatric rehabilitation field.

Irv always met me for lunch after I returned so that he could fill me in on what I missed, and also, he would joke, to "ground me" after my many days spent in altered states. After I returned home from one of my Breathwork training sessions, he called to arrange for our lunch the following day. Over the phone he joked, "Judy, I'm imagining that I'm attaching a long string to you, like on a helium balloon! Then I can keep you anchored."

The next day as I drove to meet Irv, I came to the entrance to the expressway and was amazed to see a pink balloon with a long string sitting there on the road, right in front of my car. I pulled over, got out, picked it up, and put it on the floor on the passenger side. As I re-started the engine and drove onto the expressway, the balloon immediately flew upwards and attached to the ceiling. It was a helium balloon! "Wait 'til Irv sees this!" I thought.

I arrived at the restaurant and walked in with my pink balloon. And there was Irv, already at a table. With a blue helium balloon tied to his chair! His mouth fell open when he saw me. He told me that as he was leaving to meet me, he found the blue balloon tied to a bush and thought it would make a great joke, so he brought it along. And thus we shared a meal, trying to make normal conversation, our balloons bobbing gently behind us.

What did such a synchronicity mean? It was humorous, but also profound: Irv was agnostic, a highly intellectual behavioral psychologist, and a leader in the field of psychiatric rehabilitation. As such, even though he was supportive of my quest, he had difficulty accepting or even understanding consciousness studies and spirituality. Our "impossible" synchronicity was a great shock to his worldview. And rather than dismiss it, as so many people in a similar situation might do, he courageously and with much personal effort considered it a wake-up call. He opened himself up to the "strange reality" that his friend Judith was exploring.

When Irv died about ten years later, his final professional article written as editor of a mainstream psychiatric journal took up the issue of the future of psychology. One day, he said, the field would have to acknowledge the authenticity of the spiritual experience and its relevance for mentally ill individuals. Were this to happen, he noted, *it would be the missing link for understanding the cause and meaning of mental illness.*

Irv and I had been out of contact for about three years before he wrote that article, and when I read what he had written, I felt very humbled and grateful for that strange synchronicity which apparently had radically transformed his thinking.

Our Challenge and Blessing

When we finally accept that God is everything, then we can learn to recognize the spiritual guidance that comes to us, whether inwardly or outwardly. This doesn't mean that all life problems are solved and everything becomes completely clear. There are always unknowns, confusions, and mistakes made. However, as we work through those fears, we begin to acquire an intuitive sense of a journey through life that is ours alone to follow. The challenge is to take the path that our soul recognizes, but which sometimes our ego may not.

It's easy to fall into the trap of believing that we are guiding the ship, but when we get our egos and illusions out of the way and just surrender to the God force, then life will begin to flow. The synchronistic balloon experience was, I believe, simply a teaching that there is more to know, beyond mainstream psychological and scientific explanations. This was the breakthrough for Irv. In my case, it was another confirmation that life's big lessons present themselves in ever-amazing ways.

In his youth, Carl Jung had a dream in which he was moving slowly and painfully against a mighty wind. Dense fog was rolling in all around him and as he went forward, his hands were cupped around a tiny light that threatened to go out at any moment. Jung realized that everything depended on his keeping this little light alive. And when he awoke, he realized that the light was his consciousness. Though that light at that time in his life seemed infinitely small and fragile in comparison with the powers of annihilation around him, Jung wrote that it is "the sole treasure that each and every one of us possesses." [61]

For Jung, the sense of his inner light was based on the God within. The "I" of God exists at the core of creation, within each of us. It is our challenge and blessing to reveal it.

CHAPTER 5

OUR MYSTICAL GROUND

*What good is the wisdom of the Upanishads to us,
and the insights of Chinese yoga, if we abandon our
own foundations like outworn mistakes, to settle
thievishly on foreign shores like homeless pirates?*

—Carl Jung

More than two thousand years ago, the expression of Western spirituality was divided between the Jews who called themselves Christians and who followed Jesus' teaching, and the other Jews. The Christians believed in cultivating a direct, personal relationship with God (today known as the Gnostic path). The Jews chose the existing religious doctrine of the times.

Those early (Jewish) Christians, who followed Jesus, fully accepted and fostered the mingling of the spiritual and material worlds. Tragically for the history of Western spirituality, they were marginalized because personal spirituality conflicted with Roman rule as well as with the prevailing rabbinical doctrines. This has become our Western spiritual legacy, the abiding tension between personal spirituality and religion.

In *Integral Christianity: The Spirit's Call to Evolve*, Paul R. Smith notes, "Christianity began in Palestine as an experience, it moved to Greece and became a philosophy, it moved to Italy and became an institution, it moved to Europe and became a culture, and it moved to America and became a business. *We've left the experience long behind* (my emphasis)."[62]

By leaving the experience long behind, we no longer understand that both our identity and our power to heal lies in staying connected to the primal energy of our Western spiritual source. I do not tell people which spiritual path to follow. Rather, I wish to make clear why those of us whose birth religion is rooted in the Jewish/Christian tradition need to remain open to its deep mystical influence.

Our Western Spiritual DNA

Over the years, I have encountered increasing numbers of ordinary people who are having Western mystical experiences similar to those documented by saints and mystics in the literature of the past. Such experiences were the reason I originally sought guidance, and ultimately found the work of Evelyn Underhill. I was seeking this guidance not only for myself, but also for my clients. I wanted to know why so many experiences were directly connected to the Judeo-Christian tradition. These included experiences of God, of Jesus, of Mary, and even of the Tree of Life.

Such manifestations are what I call our "Western spiritual DNA," in that Western spirituality flows from a mystical understanding of the one God. It can also come through unconditional love, forgiveness, and compassion, as exemplified by the teachings of Jesus, the Jewish rabbi. I do not believe that our spiritual DNA is merely the result of influences from culture or organized religion. Instead, I see something very different. I see evidence of the powerful undercurrents of our Western mystical ground.

"Jewish/Christian," or "Judeo-Christian" is usually understood as a solely religious term, but this is not how I am using it. I am referring to the specific way that Western civilization has had, at its foundation, a specific awareness and experience of God. When this awareness manifests and is not rejected, it transforms and heals.

The Transformative Power of Jesus

As I noted in the last chapter, personifications of the Divine provide a way for us to relate to our spiritual source. Remember, the spiritual experience is so powerful because it is more vivid, real, and unlike any other dimension of consciousness.

Why is a vision of Jesus in particular, so life-changing? My client Owen, for example, had a vision of the Sacred Heart during his Breathwork session. At the same time, he felt his own heart expand almost unbearably with love. This heart-opening led him to a direct experience of the pain and suffering that exists in the world. Because that knowledge was no longer abstract, he could not turn away. Just as the Western story tells us that Jesus took on the suffering of the world, Owen discovered his own heart's capacity for compassion and understanding. And then, with prayer and heartfelt intention, he came to realize that he could always hold pain and suffering in the Light, whether it was his own or another's. He became a kinder person, a better father and husband, and eventually a volunteer for his town's efforts to provide meals for the homeless. He maintained a private practice of prayer in order to continue to stay in touch with the powerful energy that had transformed his life.

Owen's experience was a powerful and significant event on his spiritual path. Radical transformations occur for people who accept this kind of experience. I have witnessed this even with lapsed Christians, Buddhists, Jews, die-hard atheists, and people on a New Age path. But such experiences of Jesus are too often rejected today because of ego (a need to stay in control), confusion (how could this happen? I'm an agnostic!) and/or lack of understanding (this is just brainwashing from my Catholic upbringing).

The following story exemplifies this problem. I was unable to help Ginny because of her resistance.

Rejecting the Sacred Marriage

A number of years ago, I received a visit from a woman named Ginny who wanted to see me about her ongoing depression. She was a middle-aged woman with the confidence of a successful person with a strong ego. I learned that she was a psychology professor at a nearby college and also had a private practice. She shared that she had been a practicing Buddhist for some time.

"I don't really have any specific problem," Ginny said, after we sat down. "Life is good. But I have been feeling depressed from time to time for many years and I have no idea why that should be."

I asked her if she had sought psychotherapy previously. She told me that she had been going to a "dream therapist" for many years. Hoping to help her open up, I asked her what she and the therapist had discovered. But she immediately became vague, a bit fragile, and less than enthusiastic to share. "Basically," she said, "my therapist works from a shamanic perspective and sometimes interprets according to ancient Greek symbolism, especially involving god and goddess archetypes."

During the next several meetings, I saw that Ginny was reluctant to reveal much of her background, and that confidence that I saw at our first meeting had evaporated. Not knowing how to help her I finally asked her to talk about specific dreams, since this was familiar territory to her. I hoped that her unconscious might present some clues. She responded by telling me about a recurring dream that had been troubling her for years:

"I'm alone, in a bridal gown," she said with a tremor in her voice," walking down the aisle of a church. There is bright light around me and I am always wearing a gold wedding band." Then she shrugged and said, "I guess maybe the dream is about my wish to be married or to have a relationship. But I always wake up flushed and sad afterwards."

I had a different interpretation, but rather than say anything, I asked Ginny if she had, in fact, ever been married. She
blushed a bit, said "yes" in a perfunctory way and, "I would
rather not discuss it."

"Ginny," I responded rather strongly, "I simply cannot
help you unless you are more open with me." At that point she
explained that she had been hesitant about speaking of her
past, because she didn't want me to think her unintelligent. She
explained that she had come to see me in the first place because
she had heard that I was a Ph.D. psychologist (like herself) who
was very interested in spirituality—and she believed this to be a
rare combination.

"OK," I said, "but what does this have to do with not telling
me your story?" She blushed again.

"If I told you that I was a novice Catholic nun for many
years and lived in a convent, what would you think of me?" she
stammered, the tears starting to come.

I was taken aback by her sense of shame, but then told her
that I would be very impressed to learn of her deeply religious
nature.

Ginny then told me of her childhood ambition to become a
nun, inspired by mystical experiences of Jesus when she was very
young. She grew up and fulfilled her dream, but after living in a
convent for twelve years, she realized that the holy life she had
been seeking was not to be found in that institution. "Instead,"
she said in a hushed voice, as if the nuns could still hear, "they
seemed to care more about church politics and making sure that
we got our work done."

After much anguish and struggle, Ginny made the decision to not take her final vows. Part of her turmoil included an intimate relationship with a priest that resulted in marriage after they left the church. The marriage did not last long and, with her life in great disarray and with much confusion about her next steps, Ginny decided to go back to school. She graduated with a Ph.D. in psychology. Then she began practicing Buddhist meditation. She had struggled with depression ever since.

At our next session, I shared my interpretation of Ginny's recurring dream, which I had suspected, even before hearing the details of her past, "I believe," I told her gently, "that your dream symbolizes a yearning to merge with God through the being of Jesus. It is a Sacred Marriage dream, very ancient, a powerful mystical symbolism of the soul's longing for a merging of the human and divine, a marriage between you and Jesus. When people feel such a longing in their hearts, as described in the mystical literature, it is your soul looking for its true home. When you reject those feelings, you begin to die a little inside. I believe this is why you may be depressed. You dream of walking down the aisle in a church full of light, and you are alone, with a gold band on your finger. It is your soul calling for that powerful sense of spiritual unity that you experienced in childhood with Jesus."

On hearing my explanation, Ginny immediately closed up. She had spent so many years trying to bury her past—making choices that took her as far away as possible from any hint of Catholicism. To acknowledge that original yearning would have negated the hard work she had done to construct a new identity. This new identity nevertheless remained very fragile and confused because the source of her true self was not present.

Ginny never returned for our next meeting. She also did not respond to any of my follow-up phone calls. I heard a few years later that she had given up her job and was no longer practicing psychology. And then I heard that she had spent time in a psychiatric hospital and was living on disability payments.

The kind of mystical experiences that Ginny had when young indicated that she was spiritually sensitive and had strong access to her divine nature. She sought guidance, but then turned away from that very deep part of herself when she became disenchanted with organized religion. She did not understand that the bureaucratic structures of the Catholic Church and the unfortunate actions of a priest had nothing to do with the mystical core of her birth religion. Yet deep in her soul that core knowledge remained, showing her the way to healing. Unfortunately, she and her dream therapist were rejecting the message.

I was saddened but not surprised by what happened with Ginny, because I often encounter shame and resistance in people regarding their Western spiritual heritage.

The Shame of a Religious Past

Other clients and students I work with demonstrate similar embarrassment. Lisa, for example, a very spiritually open woman discussed what she experienced during her Breathwork experience. "It was wonderful," she said, eyes shining with tears. "I was covered with white light." Then, rather hesitantly, she whispered, "and then, Jesus appeared. What was he doing there?"

Lisa and I spent months after her Breathwork discussing why she had felt such resistance toward Jesus. She describes herself as "spiritual but not religious." Her social circle also identifies itself in this way, and she admits to me that there is a shame they all feel about their childhood religion. It took much effort and courage for her to explore her spiritual roots, her ambivalence to religion, and her fears.

Saul also had a powerful Breathwork experience, but tried to ignore the most important part. He was pleased to share that he visualized himself traveling in an alien spaceship during his session. His drawing showed all the details of his vision. It included the ship traveling through a starlit deep blue universe, with pulsating silver crosses everywhere. Like Lisa and Ginny, Saul did not acknowledge any reference to Christianity. Even though I suggested how the silver crosses reflected the sacred ground of his Christian roots, he was quick to point to the historical abuses and lack of personal spirituality in his boyhood church.

Allan is unlike the others. He is not ashamed of his childhood religion. At the same time, because he is the son of a Holocaust survivor, he is afraid to acknowledge that he has been having powerful visions of Jesus, rejecting them out of hand because he is Jewish. I commented that I didn't understand his reaction because Jesus, after all, was a great Jewish spiritual teacher. Allan could only stare at me blankly.

These stories from contemporary Western seekers create much spiritual angst for them and for the people around them. They are why I believe the time has come to heal the Western soul.

The Dominance of Eastern Religions
in Psychology

After rejecting their Western spiritual heritage, Buddhism as well as influences from shamanism, have become paths of choice for many seekers. Ginny had chosen to pursue both. The influence of Eastern religions has also continued to grow in some psychology circles and also in health settings. Since the late Sixties, Buddhist meditation practices and Hindu yoga are regularly recommended for clients both in medical and in mental health institutions. They are popular both because they reduce stress and allow an individual to bypass negative and painful baggage connected with organized religion.

I certainly agree with the beneficial effects of meditation and yoga. And it may be true that Eastern religions offer a different and seemingly fresh approach to the spiritual life. However, I have found that people who actively seek a new path by denying the one into which they were born find themselves separated from the nurturing power of their spiritual ground. This influence has become so pervasive that a recent conference I attended on spirituality and psychology offered no discussion of Western spirituality and God.

Why I Encourage Western Seekers
to "Come Home"

The stories of Ginny, Lisa, Saul and Allan illustrate what I consider to be an important message in this book. In order for authentic spiritual development to occur, seekers must not turn away from their spiritual experiences. Whatever comes through the soul comes for a reason, and must be acknowledged. For example, if someone sees an image of a wolf behind closed eyes, it is important that the meaning of the wolf as a shamanic power animal be explored.

Conversely, it is necessary to recognize, acknowledge, and integrate whatever Western spiritual imagery comes through the soul and consciousness as well. What might this look like? Owen's story was an example. He accepted his vision of the Sacred Heart of Jesus, opened fully to the experience, explored the personal relevance of its meaning, and allowed it to transform his way of being in all dimensions of his life.

Seekers often will have visions in meditation or Breathwork reflecting different spiritual traditions. They will see gods/goddesses from ancient cultures, or symbols from the collective unconscious. It is a very different type of event when the energy from one's own mystical roots surfaces. For example, in Ginny's story the Sacred Marriage dream kept recurring. This was happening while she was exploring goddess imagery and dreams with her therapist and not finding any resolution for the issue that brought her tears so easily to the surface.

While all traditions reflect the same Source, spiritual development is about opening ourselves to our essence and our roots. I believe this is what the Hebrew poet Shaul Tchernichovsky meant when he wrote. "A man is nothing but the image of his native landscape."[63]

Bob's Impossible Search

Not long ago I had a thirty-year-old student I'll call Bob, who was describing his spiritual journey to my graduate human development class. He has a Catholic mother and a Jewish father, but was raised without any religious background. From the age of six he had had ecstatic, out-of-body experiences of Oneness and Light. He reached adulthood and, rather than exploring his own Western mystical roots, he headed off to Tibet and was in a monastery for two years. He could not find what he needed there, and he went to India and spent years in an ashram. After that, he went to Thailand for prolonged studies in meditation. He had very deep experiences in each of those places, and yet, he told me that he left each place feeling brokenhearted, lost, and incomplete.

"I'm feeling really confused now," Bob said, "and I don't know what to do next. I feel like my soul is being pulled towards something that is always just out of reach."

"In all of your seeking, have you ever had any experiences that reflected your Catholic mother or your Jewish father?" I asked.

Bob looked down, embarrassed, and said, "Well, I did have a sort of stigmata on my chest. . . ."

I was amazed. All of that seeking, and yet he was ignoring an extraordinarily profound mystical experience that was directly connected to his own Western heritage. Later, he came to my office to talk, and I asked, "So what did that whole stigmata experience mean to you?"

Bob looked down and shrugged, saying, "Well, I don't know."

"Have you had any other experiences of Jesus?" I asked.

"Yeah, he keeps coming," said Bob.

"Bob," I said, "Don't you think this might have some meaning for you? I don't mean to be pushing you, but I have to tell you that you are asking for help and Jesus keeps coming to you and you are rejecting Him while searching all over the world." Bob was quiet and very hesitant to accept my words. Like Ginny, he wanted his spiritual journey to take him as far away from home as possible.

Our Spiritual Identity

As a developmental psychologist, I believe that a healthy connection to our Judeo-Christian mystical roots is important. When you live out of your authentic self, you contact that extreme point where your human nature touches the Absolute. It is where your ground, your being, your identity, is penetrated by the sacred.

The developmental theorist and psychologist Eric Erikson (1902–1994) believed that human development is largely based on the quest for identity throughout the entire life span.[64] In other words, he suggests that development requires that people acknowledge and fully accept who they are, and where they come from. This means coming to terms with such influences as one's appearance, family of origin, country, sexual orientation, and gender.

While Erikson's theory on identity formation was an important contribution to contemporary developmental psychology, the area of spiritual identity is conspicuously absent from his work. At the same time, data from sociological cross-cultural research tells us that erosion of a strong cultural and spiritual identity leads to a self-image that loses its definition and becomes more fragile.[65] We become thwarted in our development if we deny an essential part of our being.

The words of Thomas Moore, well known author and teacher of Western spirituality are applicable: "Many of us spend time and energy trying to be something that we are not. But this is a move against soul, because individuality rises out of the soul as water rises out of the depths of the earth."[66] When we bypass and/or avoid a spiritual message that arises within, we are saying to the universe, "No." Instead, what we need to say is, "Yes," and not try to control what we do not understand. This, I believe, is what Tenzin Gyato, the Dalai Lama means when he says, "Study your own tradition. Much better, safer."[67]

Once again, I emphasize that all spiritual paths ultimately lead to the same place. No spiritual tradition is superior to another. But as the Hasidic rabbi Zusya (1718—1800)) said, "When I get to heaven they will not ask me, "Why were you not Moses?" Instead they will ask, "Why were you not Zusya?"[68] The wisdom in Zusya's teaching: we each have one job to do in life: to become fully, wholly and completely our true Self.

Why the Western Path is Active

From the first-hand experiences described in the stories of Abraham, Jacob, and Moses in the Old Testament, to the dreams, visions and resurrection and ascension of Jesus in the

New Testament, the essence of both Judaism and Christianity is rooted in direct, personal experience of God. As described in the previous chapter, we seek God through a personal relationship with the transcendent Other.

It is the nature of surrender to this Almighty God that is very challenging for the Western seeker. Why? Because the individualistic ego is entrenched in the personality. In the West, children begin a very conscious training to be individuals, even in infancy. Children are constantly asked to consider what their needs and desires might be: Do you want chocolate or vanilla ice cream? Do you want to stay home or come along to the store? Do you want to wear the red socks or the blue ones? Typical Western parenting experts coach parents in how to help their children make good choices and learn the consequences of bad ones.

The importance of choice also plays out in our belief that, for example, health or a cure comes from taking the right medicine, having the right surgery, or committing to good personal efforts, such as engaging in self-help practices. We learn that there is a right and wrong or good and bad way of looking at things. We have to seek out and choose a meaningful life. We are born with the sense of a "calling," and the need to formulate and follow a life mission. Further, our propensity to make choices means that, in cases of conflict, we tend to look for a solution based on the origins of the dilemma.

This individualistic and dualistic mindset is very different from the collective mentality of the East. It is also different from an emphasis on the illusory nature of life and the practice of emptying the mind in Eastern meditative practices. In the East, the concept of personal choice has been traditionally subsumed for the needs of the group. Consequently, letting go of ego in the East is not difficult. There is also comfort and security in the knowledge that surrendering to the guru is the conduit for surrendering to the Divine.

There are further implications, which underscore one of the most important distinctions between Western and Eastern consciousness and spirituality.

Because we are trained from childhood to make choices, our greatest challenge on the path is to let go of that sense that we need to be in control and instead "allow" God to flow into our lives. The Hasidic rabbi of Kotzk (1787–1859)) once asked: "Where is the dwelling place of God?" His learned students laughed. "What a thing to ask! Is not the whole world full of God's glory?" The rabbi answered his own question: "God dwells wherever a person lets God in!"[69]

Eastern spiritual traditions teach that there is no dualism in reality and meditative practice is about overcoming the illusion of that split. But our choice-making imprint, which is the basis of Western individuality, means that our spiritual task is to become fully aware of the dualities in life and become clear on how these splits play out within us. *Our spiritual path is therefore active rather than passive.*

The One God

It is not possible to talk about Western spiritual consciousness without saying something about the rift between Judaism and

Christianity. Having spent years contemplating this topic, I believe it is important for both Christians and Jews to acknowledge a basic misunderstanding that they hold, namely, the belief that our faiths developed independently of one another. On the contrary, Judaism and Christianity emerge from the same religious tradition, that of ancient Israel. As such, both Jews and Christians identify themselves as children of the same God. The entire scope of Jewish history is that of a people dominated by a certainty of and a sense of obligation to God, and Jewish spiritual consciousness can be summed up in the prayer *Shema:* "Hear O Israel, the Lord our God, the Lord, is one."

Most Western spiritual seekers don't think about the mystical roots of Judaism or Christianity. Both the Old and New Testaments are full of such events. Jesus' initial journey to mystical Union with God began with his baptism by John the Baptist. Here, Jesus saw heaven open and heard the voice of God saying, "This is my beloved Son, in whom I am well pleased."[70]

The English minister Joshua Abelson (1873–1940) wrote in *Jewish Mysticism* about the "sudden and unexpected inrushes of Divine inspiration which seized the Old Testament prophets; Isaiah's vision of a God 'whose train filled the Temple'. . . the ecstasy of Ezekiel, lifted from off his feet by the Spirit. . . ." He noted that "all these represent a stage of first-hand, living religion, to which the name of mysticism is rightly and properly applied." [71] But Abelson considered the mysticism of the Old Testament only "scaffolding" for the development of a much deeper and more involved esoteric knowledge. In late classical antiquity this knowledge culminated in the creation of the

Jewish Kabbalah, a set of mystical teachings about the relationship between the eternal and mysterious power of the All and
the mortal and finite universe. The earliest kabbalistic text, the
Sefer Yetzirah, is usually dated between the third and sixth centuries AD.

The Ever Important Question

Who is Jesus? This question often stalemates many seekers,
evoking longstanding tensions between Jews and Christians
and between the "spiritual" versus the "religious." The life of the
Buddha doesn't receive such scrutiny. The story of his life for
most Western seekers stands on its own merits as an important teaching. It is understood that he was a man who embodied
divine energy, and became a great spiritual teacher. He also is a
symbol of the journey from ordinary human understanding to
divine awareness.

Comparably, the story of Jesus the man tells us that he was
born among religious, God-fearing people and he understood
the Jewish temple to be God's home. He accepted and loved it as
the center of his peoples' religious life.[72] After John the Baptist
had baptized him in the waters of the Jordan, Jesus resisted
temptation during his forty-day vigil in the desert, and then
began his public ministry.

From that time on, Jesus, the Jewish spiritual teacher, began
to proclaim his message: *Turn your lives around; the reign of God
is approaching.*[73] This means coming home to a God-centered
awareness not in some faraway place or afterlife, but in the

immediacy of the present moment. He was speaking of an awakened awareness, a remembering of the authentic self.

As I have said, when Jesus arises in a person's consciousness, it is from the very core of our Western mystical ground. Jesus' story is a metaphor for the journey each individual soul must undergo. His assertion that "The Kingdom of God is Within" is the call for inner transformation. Ego death is symbolic of the crucifixion and spiritual rebirth is the resurrection.

This explains, I believe, why Jesus appears so often in the consciousness of people born in the West, both Christians and Jews. It is what makes a human being another Christos, an awakened child of the Creator. Deep in the soul, this healing message resounds. No matter which religion we were born into, which church or synagogue we attended, who we are or what we now might believe—it is direct, from the Source of All.

The Kabbalah and the Duality of Good and Evil

While many Western mystics portray God as loving and benign, the Kabbalah expands on this premise and provides a very deep teaching about a core issue in Western religion, that of good and evil. I will take this up in greater detail in the next chapter.

The word Kabbalah means "to receive," referring to a revelation from God received by the Jews and passed to succeeding generations through oral and written tradition for more than 1500 years. Its teachings deal with such mystical topics as dreams, meditation, automatic writing, altered states of awareness, and the mind-body relationship. It also deals with body

108 Healing the Western Soul

postures, awakening intuition, prophetic qualities, and the attainment of spiritual transcendence. In the Kabbalah, we also encounter the Tree of Life that symbolically shows humans the way back to God. It is a divine structure that shows the duality in human consciousness. At the highest point on the tree, there is a divine light greater than any living being could bear, and at their other extreme, God's presence is obscured to allow for the possibility of evil. Yet God's will is present at all levels. [74]

This is one of the deepest teachings of Judaism. It is the proof that unity with God will come precisely when the existence of duality, with all of its contradictions, is understood.

This teaching is so powerful it has given the Jewish people the strength to survive horrific anti-Semitism, pogroms and holocausts throughout history. Because God is One, the dualities of good and evil, light and dark, are part of this One.

Madly in Love with the Same God

While writing this book, I came across this verse by St. Thomas Aquinas (1225–1274), which so perfectly expresses the intent of this chapter for Jews and Christians and for all people around the world:

Our hearts irrigate the earth.
We are fields before each other.
How can we live in harmony?

First we need to know
we are all madly in love
with the same God.

—St. Thomas Aquinas (1225–1274)[75]

We are all connected to the same Source, as this beautiful verse tells us. Yet the path of the Western seeker must include the task of making a choice between the energies of good and evil wherever it exists, both within the self and without.

Thus, the difficult question: how do we know that evil is real?

CHAPTER 6

LIGHT AND DARKNESS

*I am the Lord and there is none else. I form the light
and create darkness.*
*I make peace, and create evil. I the Lord do all these
things.*

—Isaiah 45:6-7

Early in my career, I believed that the concept of Light was a
nice way of talking about peoples' positive qualities. In terms
of darkness, I subscribed to the postmodern view that there
had to be a sociological or psychological basis, such as poverty,
early childhood trauma, or emotional deprivation, for cruel and
malicious behavior to occur. Today I believe that both light and
darkness, which are synonymous for good and evil, have a much
deeper meaning than I had originally thought. As a consequence
of studying world history, having my own spiritual experiences,
working as a psychotherapist with abusers and their victims,
with ordinary people and students, with spiritual seekers, with
people experiencing psychosis, as well as with German descendants of Nazis, I have come to believe that light and darkness

have real spiritual power. I will speak first about darkness, since this aspect of human nature is perhaps most challenging for people to understand and accept.

Sybille

I met Sybille the first year I began to conduct Breathwork workshops in Germany. She had blondish grey hair tied in a neat bun and impressed me immediately as an intelligent, articulate psychiatrist. She greeted me with warmth at the beginning of a five-day retreat. Like many adults who had been caught in Hitler's twisted agenda, she was now seeking to resolve parts of her Nazi heritage that had tormented her for decades.

Two hours into the first session, Sybille was writhing on the floor, her fists tightly clenched and her face in a ferocious grimace. She was screaming, "Heil Hitler!!"

As I walked over, my stomach in a tight knot, my translator Julia ran towards me as if to protect me. At the same time, Sybille suddenly stood up and began marching smartly in place, shouting out in German, her voice high and harsh, each word sounding like a pistol shot.

"What is she doing? What is she saying?" I asked Julia. She shook her head vehemently. I pressed her to tell me. She put her hand on me as she said in a choked whisper: "I'm sorry, Judith. Sybille is screaming that she is crushing Jewish bones."

I had to excuse myself. I eventually returned, attempted to put the incident out of my mind, and got through the rest of the week. Sybille thanked me at the end of the retreat for allowing her to release old, pent-up darkness, but it took months before I could think clearly about the incident. I kept asking myself how I, as a Jew, could presume to help someone like Sybille when it seemed that her wish, deep down, was to crush the bones of my people. Where was my loyalty? Was I being the ultimate victim again, like the Jews were in the Holocaust? I prayed and asked for guidance.

A while later, I learned that Sybille had been a member of the Hitler Youth movement. This was the compulsory school system that indoctrinated thousands of children as part of Hitler's plan to create a new "master race" that would rule the world. After I read some of Hitler's writing in his *Mein Kampf*,[76] I realized what had been done to her young soul:

> My teaching is hard. Weakness has to be knocked out of them. In my "Ordensburgen" (Hitler Youth) a youth will grow up before which the world will shrink back. A violently active, intrepid, brutal youth; that is what I am after. It must be indifferent to pain. There must be no weaknesses or tenderness in it. I want to see once more in the eyes the gleam of pride and independence of the beast of prey . . . [and] eradicate the thousands of years of human domestication. Then I shall have in front of me the pure and noble natural material. With that, I can create a new order . . .[77]

Sybille had been deeply affected by the savage brainwashing that consumed her psyche in early childhood and which continued to live in her unconscious many years later. In retrospect, I realize that it was deeply courageous for her to dare to revisit that terrible time in her past. When she faced the darkness deep within her, she was able to transform it to light and be healed. I also had to face my own fears of working with descendants of Nazis and, as a result, my own darkness, as manifested in anger and anxiety, was dissolved. When I prayed for guidance, I received it. Like Sybille, I was healed of the terror as well.

Much of my work in Germany today is focused on helping children and grandchildren of Nazis deal with their cultural legacy of guilt and shame from the Holocaust. This unresolved energy literally "casts a shadow" over their lives. Thus, it is possible to see that we can be affected by darkness that is not our own, and might have even occurred before we were born. For example, families with a history of suicide or alcoholism have a collective shadow that can pass down through the generations unless it is faced and resolved. Families who have relatives who have committed crimes or who have died by violence also struggle with issues of identity and often question whether they carry a "bad gene."

Sybille's experience in the Nazi youth was certainly more treacherous than the experiences that most of us encounter in our lives. At the same time, we can all think of someone, who for no clear reason, has been negatively affected by darkness, such as a friend who was victimized or abused. It could also be a personal experience, like cruelty or abuse in the workplace. Rape, drugs, kidnapping, child slavery, or a new sport called "knockout" where a helpless person is randomly beaten for no reason at all, are all possible. There could be a catastrophic war or betrayal by a close friend or partner. How does one make sense of the horrific news of pain and suffering that saturates our consciousness daily?

Many people fall into depression, perceiving life as one tragedy after another. Or they live their lives in fear, building an arsenal of guns in their homes. Some believe there is no goodness in the world and that "God is dead." Others deny that evil exists at all, suppressing their questions about the meaning of life, focusing instead on the Fritz Perls' "Do your own thing" relativistic view, while deep down there is an undercurrent of dread.

The Reality of Evil

In the PBS video *Faith and Doubt at Ground Zero,* I heard a description of evil that particularly resonated with me, It was, "We can recognize someone as evil when she/he is unable to see humanity in someone else."[78] Certainly we can apply this definition to the person who intentionally hurts another. We can also apply it when one group of people regards another group as unacceptable and inhuman. Throughout time, we have witnessed how such behavior creates genocides, holocausts, and "crimes against humanity." We can also see evil in the mass murders that have been occurring in American schools, in movie theaters, and in places of everyday living and also in Europe, such as the 2011 massacre of 77 people, including children, in Norway.

In spite of all this, there are still many in our culture who reject the possibility that evil is a real force that can affect their lives because it cannot be scientifically proved. The postmodern view is that evil in its own right does not exist because there are no truths or absolutes. Everything is influenced by everything else. If someone does an evil deed, such as abusing another person, the relativistic, postmodern response would be that the abuser was probably abused as a child, and this is what caused the behavior. Another view is that evil cannot exist because what we consider evil in our culture might be viewed differently in another culture. Many in the New Age movement who follow Buddhism, for example, do not acknowledge that evil exists. They believe, instead, that evil is merely a concept based on dualistic thinking, which is an illusion.

Western Dualism

In the last chapter, I shared the Kabbalistic teaching of the Tree of Life: "Since God is One, the dualities of good and evil, light and dark, are part of this One." Light and darkness, births and deaths, exist in nature and are all experienced throughout life in our consciousness, in our relationships, and in our environment. In physical development and also in inner development, we are always within cycles of growth, change, and transformation.

Western mystics throughout history have realized that spiritual growth is achieved through "Purification of Self," which is about recognizing the opposing forces, both creativity and destruction, and light and darkness, within you and in others. On a spiritual path, it is impossible to move forward without accepting the reality that the force of darkness is ever-present. But the path is not a passive one; it is active. It is about accessing the light in the soul and using that light to fight the darkness. Jesus' words on the Cross, "Father, forgive them, for they know not what they do," is the great teaching about light and dark. Jesus saw evil and then saw beyond it and found forgiveness in the light.

In his classic work "Study of History," historian Arnold Toynbee describes the rise and decline of twenty-three civilizations. His overarching analysis was that spiritual challenge means that a choice must be made between light and darkness. He believed this was the reason for the robustness or decline of a civilization. He also made reference to how this historical *premise* is analogous to the decisions that individuals make regarding their own spiritual development.[79]

As a developmental psychologist, I agree with Toynbee. I have seen how the quality of people's lives seems to reflect the ways in which they deal with their own light and darkness. When people acknowledge and access their soul's light in order to face and confront their "inner darkness" (in its form of anger, fear, envy, etc.), such "spiritual warriors" seem to flow with life in easier and more fulfilling ways.

What if Inner Darkness Prevails?

A client recently asked me what happens to our soul's light when inner darkness prevails? It is a question that in large part remains a mystery. I have come to believe that inner light will be dimmed when poisonous and destructive emotions and fears take hold of a person's consciousness. Then he or she loses a connection to light, or is unable to find one. The more negativity, the more one's inner light flickers. Perhaps there comes a point when the soul's light may even be extinguished or covered up by darkness and, therefore, be out of reach of the person. And when this happens, whether it is for moments, for hours, or for the balance of a person's life—there is evil. Such a person may begin to self-destruct, engage in evil acts, and ultimately may in fact become evil.

The Power of Intention

For another perspective on good and evil as inherent forces, we can look at the power of intention. Quantum physics says that everything in the universe is energy: dynamic, interconnected, and relational. Energy manifests in life through thoughts, emotions, love, hate, good, and evil. They affect the individual self and others as well. Animals, dogs and cats being the most common example, can sense when a person has good or bad intentions, which is why they are so valued as companions and protectors. We humans are less sensitive, but even so, many people speak of their "sixth sense," an intuitive ability to know whether there is the potential for good or ill in a person or situation.

I believe that the kind of energy that a person projects, or intends, depends on their level of commitment to it. A true musician commits to a life of devoted practice in order to become one with the music. A dancer practices to become one with the dance. A Tai Chi master will spend a lifetime practicing full commitment to the movement of chi in the body, to become a vehicle through which chi can move freely. A person giving his or her life to God is committing the entire self—mind, heart, soul, and body—in order to become a channel through which God energy can freely move. When the level of commitment is that complete, there is a power released that can heal, inspire and transform lives. Unfortunately, depending on the intention, it can also destroy.

About Choice, Commitment and Partnership with God

If a seed is planted under a rock, it will still try to grow towards the sun. In the same way, I believe that each of us is born in God's Light, radiant and pure, and with the vital seeds of our potential alive in our soul. It will push us to grow, develop, and bear fruit, even under the most daunting circumstances. What then is the difference between plants and humans?

What the plant does out of its own light-seeking nature, we must achieve by choice. Choice is a commitment to bringing a certain energy into oneself and into one's environment. The deeper the commitment, the stronger the energy. The little child who accidentally drowns a kitten by too zealously giving it a bath has not done an evil deed, because he or she does not understand the consequences of such an action. But whenever the individual is capable of making a conscious, intentional choice, the possibility of joining with darkness enters the picture.

In the last chapter I talked about the act of making choices as a uniquely Western aspect of the spiritual path. Choosing is also about commitment of the whole self, the soul; it is the same energy. This is why the spiritual path is about purification. In the end, one knows with every fiber of one's being that Light is not an abstraction. It is a living force given to all humans by God, which can have a profound effect on one's own life and on the lives of others.

At the beginning of this book I spoke about a great paradox in spiritual development. When inner Light is activated, its nature is such that it cannot easily coexist with any energy that is less than pure. To give one example, when a liar admits a lie and genuinely asks for forgiveness (as opposed to hoping for personal advantage), he or she is shining light on his/her darkness. Similarly, when Sybille opened herself to accessing her unconscious identification with Nazism, she was attempting to purge its evil from her soul. Thus, the more one intentionally seeks to know God, the more the shadow parts of the personality are pushed to the surface of consciousness. Then it must be faced and dissolved. Such a partnership may come about in several ways, through meditating on one's inner light, asking for guidance, or praying for spiritual protection.

To be ethical and discerning is an essential human task. There may be times when we need spiritual counsel from someone who has spent more time "walking the walk." I don't believe we can always fight evil by ourselves. Ultimately, however, we cannot look to institutions and authority figures for definitions of right and wrong. We have to struggle with these questions and experience when something feels life-giving and when it feels destructive. While sometimes there may not be clear answers, it is still crucial to continue probing further and refining our judgments more precisely.

By partnering with the Light, we come back into accord with our divine template, which is to heal, grow, and fulfill our unique life purpose. It is both naïve and arrogant to believe that darkness can be overcome by purely psychological or rational means. Choice and commitment are not intellectual exercises but belong in the heart and soul.

When People Cannot Accept Their Inner Light

I have worked with many people who could not accept the reality of their inner light because they did not believe themselves capable or worthy of such a connection with God. This especially holds true for those who have a diagnosis of mental illness. It is much easier (and less risky) for such people to describe their experiences of darkness, demonic voices, and terrifying visions. It's a different story when I ask my clients how the Light appears to them. They are often startled, and abashed. They ask me, "How did you know?"

About ten years ago, I had a client named Janice who had been diagnosed with both bi-polar and schizo-affective disorders—two very serious diagnoses. A psychiatrist had put her on anti-psychotic medication, but the voices inside did not go away. She was in danger of losing her job as a fashion designer.

In many cases, anti-psychotic medication only dulls the voices (patients call their meds "emotional strait jackets") and does not eradicate them. Many who struggle with mental illness have learned not to talk about their experiences out of the fear that their medication, which has side effects like weight gain, tremors, sexual dysfunction, and a sense of being under a dark cloud, will be increased.

Janice was a lovely-looking 42-year-old divorced woman with shoulder-length dark hair and deep blue eyes, but her face was grey with fear and exhaustion when she came to my office.

"There are three voices," she told me, "Two are male and one female. They laugh at me, call me stupid, and tell me to cut myself, and not to listen to anything that you say."

I asked her why they didn't want her to listen to me, and she replied that they warned her that I am a bad influence.

"That's not true," I told her. "I only want you to feel better. Do you believe me?"

She hid her face in her hands and mumbled, "I don't know what to think."

"Janice," I said, "I think you really do know what to think. These voices are coming through you from a very dark place. Why else would they call you insulting names and ask you to cut yourself?"

"Because I'm an evil person, and I need to be punished." Her voice was low and desperate.

I told her that I did not believe that she was evil, or that she should suffer. Unlike an evil person, I said, I experienced light, rather than darkness in her.

I saw her eyes glaze over and she seemed to disappear inside herself.

"Janice, where are you now? Why don't you respond to what I just said?"

"They are talking to me again."

She told me her voices were saying that I should shut up.

"Don't listen to them, Janice," I said. "They know about your inner light, and that's why they don't want you to hear me."

"Do you really believe I have this light in me?" She became more alert, seeming shy and vulnerable as she considered this thought.

"I don't just believe it, I know it," I said, "And deep down, you know it too."

I told her that she did not have to listen to me, but instead suggested that she "ask the Light if it is there. And ask it for help."

Her eyes now were wide with interest and a dawning hope: "How do I do that?"

"Before bed tonight, ask for a dream to show you your true nature, and ask if it belongs to the Light."

Janice left with new energy in her step and the next day she could not wait to tell me her news.

"I can't believe it," she said, her face shining with relief. "A beautiful angel came to me and told me that she loved me. Then I saw an image of me smiling and her protecting me from the evil voices."

When I asked her who she thought the angel might be, she shyly replied, "I think it might be my guardian angel. I have the feeling her name is Sara."

"I'm sure this is true, Janice," I said. "And you now have her help to protect you. The more you develop a relationship with her and ask for her help against the darkness, the more you will find yourself in the Light. You can't fight the darkness yourself, Janice, that's why you have been losing the battle. Sara will be there to protect you now. Just ask for her help and you will feel her presence."

In the coming months, I watched Janice become stronger and more confident. The voices did not go away, but they were subdued, came less often, and she was able to keep her job. Three years since our first conversation, she regularly calls on Sara to keep her in the Light.

Critics of this approach will argue that Janice's guardian angel is at best a fantasy, a figment of her imagination, or evidence of psychosis. My response is that Sara's presence is a manifestation of Janice's inner light and spiritual strength. And if Sara comes through Janice's soul as a way to help her transform her turmoil and inner darkness to Light, then this is clearly a very important spiritual experience for her.

I have seen other clients respond in similar ways. Sometimes they describe a brilliant, white light; other times they see angels or a deceased loved one. Many will describe a figure in a white robe and say that it is Jesus. When I affirm their experiences, they feel supported, protected, and empowered. Then they are able to see themselves as spiritual warriors and no longer helpless victims trapped in a battle with darkness.

What Exactly are The Voices?

The issue of hearing inner voices is a long-term philosophical battleground between psychology and spirituality. The debate

centers on whether the voices are merely distortions and fanta-
sies presented to the surface mind in a concrete form, or whether
they are manifestations of some force, or spiritual power beyond
the self. I believe that they may be either of these two things—
and sometimes even both can be present concurrently.

Voices can be a deeply mystical aspect of our consciousness.
Such phenomena are usually heard or seen when the mind is in
a state of deep absorption without conscious thought, which is
the most favorable of all times for contact with transcendent levels of consciousness. Voices or visions experienced in this state
often take the form of a sudden upwelling of knowledge from
the depths of the soul.

The best way to assess such phenomena is to look at their
effects. In my experience with clients, when voices or visions
bring wisdom to those in confusion, calm those who were tormented with doubt, flood the personality with new understanding, offer guidance in moments of indecision, or confer knowledge of some area of spiritual life previously unknown, they
clearly are important to the individual's wellbeing. When they
leave the person in a more positive state, I believe they come
from light.

But what about when such experiences affect the person
negatively? Over the years, I have learned that sometimes when
people are troubled, frightened, and the voices they hear are
negative, there is the possibility that the person's unresolved
emotional issues and shadow parts are taking over their personality. However, rather than interpreting that such troublesome
experiences come solely from a diseased brain, I believe that

they reflect the person's—and the psychotherapist's—difficulty in accepting that darkness really can exist. This leaves both stuck and turning to meds as a solution for what is not understood. The mystic Carmelite nun St. Teresa of Avila, Spain (1515–1582) learned to cooperate with all her inner voices, both helpful and not so helpful. Often they provided her with wisdom and joy; other times they interfered with her plans, ran counter to her personal judgment, and forbade an action she had determined, or commanded one which appeared imprudent or impossible. As her spiritual life matured, she seems to have learned to discriminate between them. She seldom resisted them, although in the beginning it often seemed their guidance was the height of folly. They frequently involved her in hardships and difficulties, but she never questioned their source.[80]

The Problem of Living Without Commitment

The greatest problem with a postmodern viewpoint, in my view, is that it is basically about living without commitment. Since the reality of evil is denied in a postmodern worldview, many forms of psychotherapy and New Age practices will enable a person to evade his or her shadow side. When this happens, darkness is unnamed or projected onto others and the ego continues with its illusions, avoiding aligning the self with the good.

Psychotherapy is often unsuccessful for people who have been severely traumatized. A woman, for example, who has been sexually abused or repeatedly raped, will be able to heal more easily only after she is able to access and partner with her light, and use its energy to experience release and hopefully even for-giveness. The rational mind cannot provide such healing; it is always soul work.

By discounting the reality of good and evil, people who make negative choices do not have to deal with the soul conse-quences of their actions. There is no future or possibility for heal-ing in such cases, no vision and purpose for becoming a striving, evolving human being. I find it especially painful to witness how people with diagnoses of mental illness are adversely affected when the existence of good and evil is denied by psychology and popular culture. I say this because so much of their inner strug-gle (what psychiatry attributes to psychosis) is about healing the split between good and evil—a split that is tearing the soul apart.

A Case in Point—Mental Illness or Mental Neglect?

In 2013, a man named Aaron Alexis massacred 12 people at a Navy yard near Washington, D.C. The media will continue to puzzle out his motives. My interest is not in analyzing his sit-uation. There is much that remains unknown and it would be irresponsible to base my argument on what is gleaned from the media. However, there are key elements in his story that can be addressed from the perspective of this book.

To begin with, it appears that he was engaged in two polar opposite practices: he was regularly expanding his conscious-ness in Buddhist meditation and he was also regularly going into an altered state because of an addiction to violent video games.

According to CNN, Alexis contacted two Veterans Affairs hospitals for help with insomnia and hearing voices. He also told police that individuals were following him and sending vibrations into his body.[81]

Clearly Aaron desperately needed both emotional and spiritual support. He reached out and was put on psychotropic medication. This medication did not help Aaron nor did it prevent the killings. There was no recognition that Aaron's inner and outer reality was split between light and darkness. He needed assistance in healing the split so that he could recognize what was happening to him.

In certain ways, Aaron's story is very similar to that of James Holmes, the man who perpetrated the Colorado movie theater massacre in 2010. Holmes, a Ph.D. candidate in neuroscience, was reported to be very interested in altered states and was also addicted to violent video games.

Were I to work with persons such as Aaron and James, I would begin by trying to get them to recognize what they were dealing with; I would tell them that they were opening their consciousness to two very powerful opposing energies of light and darkness. I'd ask whether they saw the situation this way and if they did, I'd want to know what choice they were going to make. I would make no bones about calling their struggle by its true name, an internal warfare between good and evil. My message would be, "If you want to stay in the light that you experience in your lives—in Aaron's case, the Buddhist temple, in James case, his productive academic career—you have to actively engage, show up, recognize what you are doing and make a conscious commitment as to which direction you are going to take."

If Aaron and James decided to choose the Light, then they would need to intentionally align their whole selves with the Light and bring it forth when those dark voices came to them. They would need to have an active practice like prayer or meditation to help them stay in this Light. In both their cases, they would need a spiritual guide to be there with them and to point out when they begin to falter.

Providing medication is not the answer. Both men were on medication that clearly had no effect. They were engaged in a huge struggle within the soul that was rapidly escalating. Evil is a real force, an immensely powerful and destructive force. Psychiatry, psychology, and our entire culture needs to start to deal with it as such.

What if the Darkness Seems too Strong?

Sometimes people become blocked because they are unable to understand or move through their shadow issues. Psychology and popular culture generally refer to this state as depression, anxiety, or as existential emptiness and despair. Other times people feel blocked because they have difficulty recognizing the shadow in a personal relationship or in their connection with a certain group. I have heard from a client, for example, "He treats me badly, but I also know that there is light and goodness in him." Yes, we all have goodness. But this does not negate the pain that darkness can create in another and which cannot be ignored without blocking one's own development.

In such difficult situations, I often recommend the following as a way of keeping one's energy clear and aligned with the Light:

- Choose a spiritual method, whether Breathwork, dream work, or activities such as meditation, walking in nature, listening to music, whatever helps a person connect to inner light and feels personally healing;

- Ask the Light (however one conceptualizes it) for guidance about what needs to be faced;

- It can be especially helpful to ask for clarity before sleep and to be open to answers that come in dreams; record these in a journal and reflect on their meaning.

A state of being blocked may also mean that outside help is needed from a spiritually-oriented therapist, guide, or community. Psycho-spiritual work can be particularly important, in such cases, because sometimes everything seems very obscure and confusing just before awareness arrives. It is always helpful to consider whether there is a greater meaning that we have not yet grasped.

There is the saying: "Man does not pull himself up to heaven by the hair."[82]In other words, sheer willpower is not going to solve the problem; instead, one has to remain open to receive the answer. I have always found that "when the student is ready, the teacher appears," whether through a person, a book, a dream, an insight, or a moment of grace. Much of my life has been guided in just such a way. It is also true that sometimes the only thing to do is to trust, to surrender to God, and to allow the answer to appear in its own time.

But what to do if there is darkness for what seems like a long period of time? "You must not give up," I tell people.

Creativity Through a Struggle with Darkness

Some people seem able to be more creative, intuitive, and spiritually open than others. Psychologists who study creativity typically debate whether "nature or nurture"—a quirk of genetics or a supportive environment, for example—is the determining factor. While psychology's reference points are important, they are not the whole story. Some works of art or great athletic accomplishments, for example, are so astonishing and inspiring that we know without a doubt that the individual responsible was connected to a spiritual energy beyond ordinary human capacity.

But what about the creativity that inspires even when it seems to come from inner angst and not from inner light? Many songs and works of art, for example, result from a lengthy struggle with unresolved issues of pain and longing. It is through the artist's heroic expression of pain that room is made for the light to shine forth. Some artists do not realize this, and they remain tortured throughout their lives. In such cases, we are the ones who benefit from their courageous quest to express truth, because such a quest for healing is contagious, serving as an example and a source of energy to bring people together. Hede's story is a moving example of this quest.

Transforming Hitler's Legacy

Hede was in her sixties when I met her in Germany years ago.

I learned that she had spent most of her adult life tormented by concerns that some of her close relatives were active in the Nazi party. As a way of coming to terms with this possible legacy, she spent years traveling to different synagogues in America, trying to tell the Jewish people her story as a Nazi child. Sometimes they cried, realizing that a German child can also be a victim. Other times, they turned away from her.

I first met Hede on one of my first trips to Germany. She joined a pilgrimage to Auschwitz that I led with my colleague Ingo Jahrsetz. For a week, our group of twelve participants and Ingo and I spent each day in the camp, and then came together in the evenings to process feelings. During one of those evenings, Hede told us that several years earlier, during meditation, she had suddenly remembered a frightening Hitler vision that she had had first had when she was around six years old.

I asked Hede to describe it, and she began by explaining that it was very common during the Third Reich for Hitler to be paraded down the avenues in a big limousine while thousands of frenzied people would cheer and shout, "Heil! Heil!" Her vision related to those times:

> As the float passed, Hede was terrified to see Hitler
> holding in front of him the horns of a severed head
> of a bull. Blood was pouring from its neck. Her gaze
> was drawn upward to a dark and malevolent-look-
> ing angel, high in the sky above the float. It was hold-
> ing very long strings that were attached to Hitler's
> arms and legs. The angel was pulling the strings.
> Hede began to sob as she told us this story and she

*asked, "What could this mean? Why does it haunt
me so?"*

Hede understandably became emotional as she told us this
story. I told her that I believed that her child's soul recognized
that an evil energy was not only acting through Hitler, but also
manipulating his actions. Hede and the others were quiet after
my interpretation, and in retrospect I have come to realize that
many educated Europeans, and especially Germans, reject anything to do with religion. I think this is partly because Hitler
made Nazism a spiritual movement; the German people were
considered to be beings of light while other groups of people,
and especially the Jews, were considered dark and subhuman.

In order for our German participants to discuss evil as if it
were real, it was necessary to acknowledge that there was spiritual meaning to it. And then to recognize how this spiritual
meaning is related to the horrors of the past. This was not easy
to do. Hede, however, had the courage and determination to try.
And this courage can consistently be observed in the actions she
has taken over the years.

Before I met Hede, she had taken it on herself to visit the
concentration camp Mauthausen in Austria. While there, she
had been so overwhelmed by the atmosphere of unspeakable
suffering that she had fallen to her knees to pray. An inner
prompting urged her to look up and, high above the camp, she
had seen a radiant light of unearthly beauty shining over the
whole complex, emanating heavenly peace and love. She heard a
voice say, "This is a place of initiation." Her following words give
testament to her experience:

A sudden shift in perception made me see that this place of terror was almost a sacred place—a holy place of compassion where we can fully experience the lowest of the low and rise to the most high. A place of truth where we all can learn to face that whatever happens on this planet is in all of us. This can bring us to a new level of understanding from which reconciliation is possible, and to a place of wholeness where we can open to a new spiritual way of being. A place where Germans and Jews can come together, grieve together, pray together, and enter together into the healing light.

A few weeks later, she spontaneously turned on the radio after waking from a heavy and disturbed sleep. As the sounds of Bach filled the room, she was filled with love and inspiration. But then she heard a voice asking her to turn around, and she saw a vision of the earth, covered with victims of the Holocaust. She heard their screams of agony. She began to sob uncontrollably, even while realizing that both extremes were her German heritage, and that "accepting in us the most horrible darkness is the only way for the light on this planet to be born."

She took up pen and paper and words poured out of her pen, which in her opinion came from another realm. When she had finished, the poem to the Jewish people, became part of her healing process:

Jerusalem Is Waiting

You went to the slaughterhouse knowing your fate.

You went because God needed you as a people to transcend pain, horror, and death.

You went there knowing that one day you would have to forgive, because only forgiveness can open the heart of the planet.

You went because you, "the chosen people," the caretaker of the heart, needed to demonstrate forgiveness and love for us all to see.

You went there to say, like Joseph to his brothers, "You meant it for evil but God meant it for good."

You went there to bring resurrection to your people and the world.

You went there to show that one can be lifted, unscarred, from Hell to Heaven so that the Messiah can be born in all Humanity.

You went there to transcend duality through the understanding that devil and angel are each one side of the same.

You went there to overcome hate and learn to love all human beings, regardless of color, race, or nationality.

You went there to make way for the new human being, created in wholeness, neither victim nor executioner.

*You went there because only your forgiveness can
bring the Messiah to Jerusalem.*

*You went there to carry out a cosmic task, to open
Jerusalem, the heart of the planet, for all humanity.*

You went there...the Messiah is waiting.

Hede finally understood through her poem that everything
is connected—light and dark, good and evil, high and low. She
realized that she now had to embrace (and if possible, even love)
it all.

Most recently, when she and I communicated, she said to
me; "it just shows Judith, the very difficult and demanding path
we all have to travel. I knew then, and I know now, that I still
have a long way to go to integrate it all. But what I can say for
sure—is this healing path is a blessing."

We must not lose sight of Hede's vision of the "new human
being," created in wholeness. Our most important task is to
acknowledge light and dark energies and learn how to work
with that knowledge consciously and ethically, to become the
spiritual heroes we are born to be. But first, we have to wake up.

Part Three

OUR WESTERN SPIRITUAL PATH

CHAPTER 7

STAGE ONE: SPIRITUAL AWAKENING

Man's being...is not only given to him but also demanded of him.... He is asked to make of himself what he is supposed to become, to fulfill his destiny.

—Paul Tillich (1886-1965)

A 45 year-old dentist named Joe was in an automobile accident, a collision at a four-way stop with another driver. It was not clear who was at fault. Fortunately, he was basically okay, but his car was totaled. The other driver suffered serious injuries and was in rehab, unable to return to work. Even though each of the respective insurance companies had agreed on a settlement, Joe was feeling very concerned about the other driver and guilty over his part in the accident. His wife, family, and friends were supportive and challenged him about his self-recriminations, but nonetheless he remained upset.

Some weeks later, Joe called me. Sounding panicked, he said that he had to see me right away. He told me that he believed that the accident had caused a "mental illness," because very serious and frightening things were happening to him. In person, he turned out to be a nice-looking man, poised, polite and friendly, and not as agitated as he had been over the phone. After spending some time meticulously checking out my academic credentials, he then asked for assurances that what he told me would be kept confidential. When I inquired what exactly his self-described mental illness looked like, he began to share, almost in a whisper:

"Suddenly, for the first time in my life, I am having crazy dreams," he said. "I see bright colors, white light, and I even saw an image of what looked like Jesus. Not only that, but I seem to know things before they happen. Like just last week, I had a dream about my old college roommate, whom I haven't seen in 20 years, and then the next day after the dream, I bumped into him in the elevator of my office building."

As Joe described these events, he lost his calm demeanor, his face reddened, and he appeared on the verge of tears. "Something even happened this morning," he said, "as I was preparing to come and see you. I suddenly heard the Christmas carol 'Silent Night' in my head. I didn't understand where this was coming from, since we're in July. I got into my car to come here, turned on the radio to my usual station, and what song was playing but 'Silent Night'! I was shocked; it seems that the station was celebrating a 'Christmas in July' day."

"I feel like I'm losing my mind," Joe said, "None of these experiences make any sense to me. I'm questioning my sanity, my reality, everything."

Joe was surprised that I remained so composed after hearing his story. When I shared that he was experiencing the first stage of the Western spiritual path—an awakening to knowledge of a spiritual reality, he felt very conflicted. An agnostic, the recent experiences of expanded consciousness were very challenging to this rational, scientifically trained man.

The self versus the Self

I shared with Joe, Carl Jung's distinction between the self (with a small 's') and the Self (with a capital 'S') discussed in Chapter 1. The former is related to the ego and the individual personality, and the latter to the soul. After Joe heard my explanation, he became quiet and closed his eyes for a moment. Then he asked, "What does all this have to do with these weird experiences I've been having?"

"Your soul is your foundation," I told Joe, "the driving force of your life. God is an empty theological concept unless a relationship exists between your individual personality and this deep part of your spiritual nature. Your soul seeks and requires experiences of God, even though you may not be consciously aware of this deep yearning."

"Perhaps," I suggested, "this is why your dreams of brilliant light and Jesus are occurring. It may also be why you had the synchronicity of Silent Night and other experiences beyond our ordinary senses. Stage one of the spiritual journey shows us we are capable of knowing much more; it provides greater awareness about the true nature of reality."

"Many people have the kinds of experiences you are having, Joe. However, because they don't understand them, they often

ignore the experiences and try not to pay attention. You are taking them seriously even if they make you uncomfortable. And
that's good."

Joe was eventually able to accept my explanation, but several months passed before he began to feel more secure and
grounded. Meanwhile, his experiences of expanded consciousness continued and became even more intense. He saw me
regularly for support and guidance and eventually joined the
Breathwork group. In time, he came to understand that the identity crisis precipitated by his accident had initiated him into a
new heightened reality and begun his spiritual journey.

The Stages of Life and the Spiritual Journey

The famous "All the World's a Stage" monologue in Shakespeare's
"As You Like It" has the line, "One man in his time plays many
parts," referring to the well-known stages of life, from infancy
to childhood, adulthood, and old age. A key concept about
these stages is that each has its own unique challenge before one
can move on to the next one. Thus, the philosopher Friedrich
Nietzsche's words: "He who would learn to fly one day must first
learn to stand and walk and run and climb and dance; one cannot fly into flying."[84]

In this regard, the developmental theorist Eric Erickson
identified eight stages, each with a specific challenge that must
be addressed for healthy functioning and identity formation in
life. For example, the basic conflict in the stage of infancy (from
birth to 18 months) is about trust vs. mistrust. If the child does

not experience reliability, care and affection from caregivers, the next stage of development will not be fully achieved and there will be issues of mistrust that carry forward and create a deep undercurrent in future stages.[85]

Although Erikson did not refer to spirituality as an integral part of human development, the same principles that he cited regarding the necessity of meeting specific challenges in each life stage are applicable in spiritual development as well. Insights and personal revelations can occur even at the final moment of life. Consider the last words of Steve Jobs, reported by his sister Patty, after he looked first at his family and then past them: "Oh wow. Oh wow. Oh wow.[86]

In this chapter and the two that follow, I share what these challenges are, based on my own spiritual journey, my work with seekers, and also from extensive study of the writings of Western mystics.

The Three Stages of the Western Spiritual Path

When I first read the work of Evelyn Underhill, I was deeply interested in her description of what she called "The Mystic Way," a path of spiritual development based on the writings of saints and mystics of old. She identified five stages:

1. Awakening of Self: intense, though sometimes confusing, heightened states of consciousness, which lead to awareness of one's spiritual nature and reality;

2. Purgation: a process of "purification" to dissolve shadow or inner darkness;

3. Illumination: strong and profound mystical experiences; life becomes more God-centered, purgation continues;

4. Dark Night of the Soul: a spiritual void and seeming loss of the God relationship brings deep loneliness and despair. Now, it is time to release all attachment to the sense of having one's own separate identity, including even the identity of "being spiritual;"

5. Union: the final transformation, one has at last become free of shadow, separate identity, and ego, has merged with the Divine, and is One with All.[87]

Ira Progoff, Ph.D. (1921–1998), a leading authority on Jungian depth psychology, wrote in the forward to the thirteenth edition of Underhill's *Mysticism*:

> You may not be aware of it, but this unpretentious volume you are holding in your hands is one of the truly important books in the English language.[88]

I agree with Progoff that Underhill's contribution is seminal. She does not, however, discuss in any depth the psychoemotional challenges that Western mystics of the past faced on the path. Nor does she describe how ordinary people may travel this same path today. For these reasons, I modified "The Mystic Way" to make it more accessible to readers, reducing the number of its stages to three by including "Purgation" (or what I call "ego death") in "Awakening," and "Dark Night of the Soul" in "Illumination." I did this because, in my experience, they are actually transitional challenges before the seeker moves more fully into the next stage. This revised model of the Western Spiritual Path now looks like this:

1. Spiritual Awakening;

2. Illumination;

3. Union.

These three stages are universal in human consciousness, similar to the "Hero's Journey" described by mythologist Joseph Campbell (1904–1987) as the journey to God.[89] His model, identified in the writings of mythology and religion, have been embraced by world cultures. In the first stage of the journey, called *Departure*, the Hero begins the quest for self, which is analogous to the first stage of *Awakening*. His second stage, called *Initiation*, is the time of the greatest growth and spiritual challenge for the hero and analogous to *Illumination*. In his final stage, called *Return*, the hero re-enters society transformed by his efforts and ready to share his soul's new knowledge. This is analogous to the final stage of *Union*, which in the West is considered a spiritual homecoming back to God.

Another way to understand these three-fold developmental stages of the Western Spiritual Path is to again compare them with the creative process of the artist or musician, where that first inspiration and subsequent commitment to one's muse is followed by years of study and hard work, perseverance through failure and defeats, in pursuit of an end stage of ultimate mastery.

When we consider the artist, cloistered nun, or meditating monk, we tend to picture a somewhat linear path of discipline that will hopefully one day have a payoff. While this is true with the view through a long lens, phases of challenge and transformation occur over and over in a life span. There are always higher and higher levels to access in the journey to God, just as the artist who has become a master ultimately realizes how little he or she really knows. This is why I often say that spiritual development is less like a path and more like a spiral. Reaching Union is not about achievement, deciding to become enlightened, or figuring out how long it will take to reach this goal. It is a life-long process.

This brings us to a description of the two characteristics that typically lead to that initial spiritual awakening. One I call "A Glimpse of the Transcendent," and the other, "Asking Big Questions."

A Glimpse of the Transcendent— The First Characteristic

"A Glimpse of the Transcendent" is a spiritual experience—a vision, an unforgettable dream, a psychic or paranormal event, a near-death experience (NDE), a mystical event, or synchronicity. These are the sorts of experiences that Joe had when he first came to see me, and which readers may recognize from their own lives. As I described in Chapter One, these are messages arising in the soul, bringing knowledge of the authentic Self. The great psychologist William James (1842–1910) called such unforeseen events "invasions of consciousness."[90] As I also shared in chapter one, they are so powerful because they come through at a deep, non-rational level and do not fit with the ego's carefully constructed worldview. Awakenings can also be the result of deliberate efforts to expand consciousness, for example, as a result of engaging in prayer, meditation, or in processes like Breathwork.

Romanian scholar Mircea Eliade (1907–1986), a leading interpreter of mystical experiences, wrote that such experiences "challenge us to transform our lives." [91] H emphasized that when the sacred manifest, we are not in control of these encounters. He proposed the term *hierphany*, meaning "a manifestation of the sacred," pointing out that we first become aware of the sacred because of its dramatic contrast with everyday experience. When the sacred breaks into our secular sphere, we recognize it as "something of a wholly different order, a reality that does not belong to our world."[92]

The most important part of Eliade's contribution is that he grounds his theory of the sacred not in psychology but in reality itself, suggesting that the powerful psychological reactions we have in such encounters are due to our contact with the most "real" level of experience we can have. Calling such experiences "grace," he said the proper attitude is humility and gratitude.[93]

Dreams as a Glimpse of the "Really Real"

Early Jewish mystics maintained that dreams represent the "really real" world. Rabbi Zalman (1720-1797), known as "The Gaon" (genius) of Vilna, said: "God created sleep to this end only, that man should attain the insights that he cannot attain… when the soul is joined to the body; for during sleep, the soul is out of the body and clothed in a supernal garment."[94]

The following story is an example of how a powerful dream can be the catalyst for Awakening:

John, a rather straight-laced banker, was a forty-something man with a big heart and a loving family. Although his day-to-day work life seemed at times tedious, overall he was a happy person and enjoyed his wife and two young children very much. As a banker, his interests were pretty mainstream. He went to church occasionally, but never gave much energy to any psychological or even spiritual concerns. His widowed mother lived with the family and they all had a warm and loving relationship.

One night, John had a dream that awakened him from sleep. In the dream, he had found himself in a cemetery. But this cemetery was unlike any he had ever seen: each of the monuments was beautiful, sculptured marble. There was a small, sparkling blue ocean in the middle of the cemetery, with bountiful foliage and brilliantly colored flowers all around. Enveloping the idyllic beauty of this place, there was a pulsating golden-white light that felt incredibly strong and sacred to this secular man.

While typically, John did not analyze his dreams, he could not help but wonder what such a dream could mean. Cemeteries had always made him nervous and brought up uneasy feelings about death. His feelings after the dream, however, now caused him to view it as something almost holy, peaceful, and even miraculous.

A few days later John's mother suddenly died of stroke. As he gazed at her peaceful face, tears of gratitude ran down his cheeks as he remembered his dream. He believed it had been a gift from God, helping him to prepare and accept his mother's imminent passing, showing him that death was nothing to fear, and that his mother was now in a beautiful, loving place.

I met John about a year after his mother's death, and after he told me about the dream he said it had been a "Spiritual Awakening" for him, showing him that a sacred, loving, Higher Power is a big part of what existence is about. Over the past year he had been motivated to read spiritual literature. Now he wanted to do some personal work with me so that he could go deeper into what still felt like an incredible mystery.

A Multidimensional Reality

Dreams are but one manifestation of the transcendent. A person may also become aware that reality is not merely physical, but multidimensional: vivid colors appear when the eyes are closed, and lights and auras radiate around objects and people, making the world feel intensely vibrant and alive. There are synchronicities, like Joe's experience of "Silent Night" on the radio, or precognitive or clairvoyant events, inner voices, as well as visions of departed loved ones, or images of Jesus, Mary, saints and other holy persons. One client who was a young mother told me that she was vacuuming in the living room one day when she suddenly heard a voice shout her name with a tremendous sense of urgency. She immediately ran to the next room, where her two-year-old had been napping and discovered that he was choking on something he had swallowed. She quickly turned him upside-down, thumped him on the back, and out popped a small button. Awed and grateful for the clairvoyant message that saved his life, she initiated her Spiritual Awakening, which led to a decision to begin a practice of prayer and self-exploration.

Asking Big Questions—
The Second Characteristic

An intense yearning, a hidden longing, feelings of being pulled towards something but unaware of what that something is, can initiate what I call "Asking Big Questions." Of this state of mind, Russian esoteric philosopher P. D. Ouspensky (1878–1947) wrote, "It is only when we realize that life is taking us nowhere that it begins to have meaning."[95] When daily life and its goals and pleasures no longer completely satisfy, questions about the meaning of life, death, God, and human purpose arise within and relentlessly push for answers.

Sometimes when I meet with clients who are obsessing over a particular life concern such as a broken relationship, a problem at work, or any other difficulty that is keeping them stuck and unhappy, I ask them to go deeper. For example, when a woman named Joan told me she was so angry at her supervisor that she could think of little else, I asked her what she believed to be her life's purpose.

"What do you mean?" she asked, looking confused.

I suggested that she close her eyes, contemplate deeply, and imagine herself as an old woman at the end of her life. "How important will your supervisor be to you then, Joan," I asked. "What will you think about then, when you consider the meaning of your life?"

I have discovered that "big questions" such as the one I asked Joan, will often help people look at their life travails from a more balanced perspective. Also, when they open their minds to explore such questions, they are stretched beyond their ego concerns and become open to their soul, which can catapult them into the first stage of the Path.

"Asking Big Questions" can occur for no particular reason, or before or after a glimpse of the transcendent, or because of an identity crisis or life trauma. The search can begin early, even in childhood, which many a parent has learned when challenged to explain why a beloved pet has died. The young can astonish us with their depth and philosophical ponderings, but often such seeking fades as the child grows and acquires society's worldview.

One afternoon many years ago, I had a visit from three young people who were not so accepting of the status quo:

Three Tattooed Pilgrims

George was a 15 year-old boy who had been recently expelled from school, along with his friends Valerie and Tim. They had been acting out, skipping classes, using marijuana and other hallucinogens, and had rejected the efforts of their school counselor. Their punishment was to begin counseling with a psychotherapist and to spend time at a drug treatment clinic. They had also been sent to three different private schools to break up their friendship—without success.

After I agreed to meet with George, I heard from his mother that he was refusing to come see me. Rather than have him dragged in kicking and screaming, I called him on the phone, introduced myself and invited him to ask me anything he wanted to know, in order to decide whether a visit was worth his while. This approach seemed to break down some barriers, and as part of the agreement, I agreed to meet not only with him, but also with his two co-conspirators.

The doorbell rang right on time and I opened the door to see three young, tattooed, body-pierced kids with wildly colored spiked hair staring at me. Their attention was immediately diverted, when my Irish water spaniel Chewbacca gave them an enthusiastic greeting. A reliable judge of character, Chewie seemed to have no doubt that this uncommon trio was A-OK.

We sat in the living room, chatting informally, but it soon became apparent that this session would be different from what I had expected. I had thought they would tell me about their problems with their parents and schools, and I would encourage them to think of ways they could interact with the authority figures in their lives and keep everyone happy.

I soon learned that these three teens were not interested in this kind of discussion, but were longing for guidance and support concerning questions that no one else seemed to care about—questions that had partly arisen as a result of their drug experiences. They wanted to know about the meaning of life, death, God, and good and evil. They had not been very successful finding answers on their own, or when they had tried to communicate with family, friends, and teachers about such issues. This is why they wanted to stick together; they felt that no one else understood.

For part of the session, I affirmed their experiences: telling them that I believed that their big questions about life's meaning were a crucial part of being here in this world. Their relief was palpable. I also pointed out that they no longer had to take drugs to gain greater understanding. Rather, I suggested that they learn how to explore through their dreams, through meditation, even through reading, intuition, and reflective thinking. The key, I said, was to learn how to access their inner wisdom.

All three seemed to understand what I was saying, and we spent some time talking about their dreams. They were excited to see that there were options other than drugs for achieving self-understanding. I then suggested that we try a Breathwork session right in my living room, in order to illustrate one way that they could access their other way of knowing. They welcomed the idea and soon were lying down on foam mats, eyes closed.

I could not help but feel that we were in a sacred space as the music began and I looked at their innocent young faces under the tattoos and body piercings. The session lasted nearly two hours, and as it ended they slowly sat up and drank the cups of hot, sweetened tea that I had placed next to their mats. As I listened to them excitedly share their experiences, I could see that all three had gained a new awareness of their souls' capacities. Previously, they had believed that the richness of their inner worlds was merely drug-induced. Now, they were beginning to understand that finding answers to their deepest questions would be part of life's journey. They left, empowered by the knowledge that they could always find inner guidance by focusing within.

We came together three more times to do Breathwork, followed up by individual sessions that included family members. A decade has now passed, and I still receive Christmas cards from all three and occasionally a phone call where they fill me in on their latest plans. They no longer hang out as a trio, although they remain in contact. George graduated from a fine New England college, went to graduate school and then joined the Peace Corps. Valerie became a registered nurse in the West, and Tim married and is a high school teacher.

All three have grown tremendously, both emotionally and spiritually. They have learned to have faith in themselves, in God, and are also able to accept those who may not understand their worldview. When they get together and reflect on their past, they agree that they had always sensed that there was more to reality than what they knew. They also realize that their use of drugs was their desperate search to find that reality.

Challenges in Spiritual Awakening

There are many inspiring stories of people who have experienced a spiritual awakening. Without guidance, however, this first stage of the Western Spiritual Path can be rocky and difficult because there are some emotional challenges that are part of any shift that might occur in a person's worldviews, values, and priorities. Following are some common examples:

1. Fear of Going Crazy

Joe was very afraid that he was becoming mentally ill after his automobile accident and his first "glimpse of the transcendent," because he was well aware that society interprets the kinds of experiences he was having as signs of mental instability. Since he had almost never read any psychological or spiritual literature and was not familiar with what it meant to expand one's consciousness, he did not know that ordinary people like himself could experience Spiritual Awakenings similar to saints and mystics from the distant past.

The young college student, Craig, whom I described in the first chapter, was actively meditating, because he felt led to "ask big questions" about whether there was more to life. Despite his spiritual practice, there was much he did not yet understand about what psycho-spiritual development was really about. Then, when he began to get answers, in the form of a powerful dream about his father, he became overwhelmed and paranoid because he could not figure out how to fit the experience into his current worldview. And since the adults and professional helpers in his world were mostly ignoring his Spiritual Awakening and trying, instead, to get him "back to normal," he could only wonder if ultimately they were right to question his sanity.

2. Alienation

Since the powerful emotions that arise in Awakening are often very difficult to describe or explain, the aftermath of a spiritual experience can include feelings of loneliness and alienation. The word "ineffable," meaning "incapable of being expressed in words" applies. Isaac Luria (1534-1572), the 16th century Kabbalist mystic refused to commit his seminal teachings in written form. When his disciples pleaded with him to do so, he said, "I can hardly open my mouth to speak without feeling as though the sea burst its dams and overflowed."[95a] How then shall I express what my soul has received, and how can I put it down in a book?" Moreover, as the person attempts to come to terms with the spiritual experience, his or her behavior will seem bizarre and worrisome to friends, family, and acquaintances—sometimes with tragic results.

Some years ago, Sheila, a young married woman and mother of a toddler, went through the heartbreaking ordeal of having her husband Frank dying from cancer. As she held him in her arms, he took his final breath and she suddenly had a very strong mystical experience, a vision where her husband's entire being was transformed into brilliant white light. She immediately realized that death was not what she had believed and, as a result, she felt serene and at peace. As a symbol of what she had experienced, she began to dress in white clothing because it seemed to reflect her beloved husband's transformation into the Light. His parents and her parents were deeply shocked by her response to her loss and called for psychiatric intervention. They were good people who cared deeply about Sheila. But in their worry and grief, not only did they not allow her to attend her husband's funeral, but they had her committed to a psychiatric facility in the hope of restoring her to her former self.

Sheila was crushed by the family's decision and her inability to celebrate her husband's journey into the light at his funeral. After she returned home days later, with a regimen of medications for her "delusions," there were many months of distance and anger existing between her and her in-laws and parents.

Ultimately, because of the love they all had for the two-year-old child, they finally were able to come together and heal.

How much trauma could have been avoided if the family had been open to Sheila's experience of her husband's last moments? They also might have benefited emotionally and spiritually themselves, if they had heard what Sheila had to tell them of her mystical experience at the threshold of death.

As it happens, both the dying process and death of a loved one frequently can push people into Awakening, because death challenges us with the biggest of all questions about reality. It is not unusual to have profound experiences that are very difficult to explain to those on the outside—stories abound of visionary experiences, moments of awe and wonder, and also contact from the departed after death. Not only is there enormous psychological pressure to make meaning of the event, but above all, at the threshold of life and death, the heart can be spiritually open. Old wounds are healed, lifelong issues are resolved, and love becomes the priority and the desire to speak one's highest truth.

This is a difficult area for psychology, which tends to focus on the effects of trauma as an explanation for heightened states of consciousness, missing the transformative power contained therein. Yet many have heard people express gratitude for their suffering—whether cancer, a tornado flattening the house, or even the death of a loved one—because the result is a life enriched and the mind and heart liberated of its misconceptions.

Before people enter the stage of Spiritual Awakening, there is a common worldview with friends, colleagues, family, and the culture. But many will feel they no longer "fit" after contact with a divine reality. Not only can the shift be difficult, causing feelings of loss, alienation, and confusion, it can also have tragic consequences, as in Sheila's case.

3. Ego Loss / Ego Death

Spiritual development is about dissolving those aspects of our ego (sense of self) where we believe we are in control and where we perceive ourselves as separate beings, apart from one another and from life's natural flow. The person who believes that wealth, power, and influence are shields from uncertainty is one example of a typical mindset, which we find when the sense of self is based mainly on physical appearance, personality, and types of work and possessions. Moreover, in popular culture, the concept of ego is also often equated with conceit, presumptuousness, and a certain demanding childishness; for example, to "have a big ego" means to be self-involved and narcissistic. In this context, a person may make self-aggrandizing statements on one day, and self-deprecating ones the next. Thus, the ego's structuring of reality oscillates between a positive and a negative outlook.

All of these attempts to "be Somebody" are challenged in Awakening. There is a struggle to regain psychological equilibrium, with questions such as, "Who am I now?" "How do I behave?" "What do I believe?" "Who has the answers?" All of these uncertainties can cause intense inner conflict. Life no longer makes any sense and this can be terrifying.

4. Fear of Death

Because of the experience of ego death, many people will become haunted by feelings of actual physical death at the beginning of their spiritual journey. My client Gretchen, for example, had a number of frightening dreams in Awakening, in which she and her loved ones were in constant danger of being killed. Another client, Jeff, was 42 years old, healthy and vigorous, a successful businessman, husband, and father of two young girls. When his spiritual awakening led him to give up his successful textile business in order to work with troubled youth, this new radically different way of being precipitated a huge identity crisis and resulting ego death. Who was he now? His old self seemed to be dying. One day he told me rather despondently that he felt that he was not long for this world. He was greatly relieved when I explained that his death anxiety was common and related to this stage of ego and identity loss, and not to his physical body.

Resolving the Challenges in Awakening

When I work with people who are experiencing the challenges of the first stage, I tell them that there are two ways to move forward and they need to do both in order to feel better. They need to trust and surrender to the healing process awakening within and, they need to commit to the work ahead.

As I have said, there is a tremendous dissonance with the loss of ego, one's identity and worldview, especially because most people need to feel in control and their anxiety demands immediate gratification—namely, that the discomfort goes away. It is not easy to understand that instead of giving in to this need, it is necessary to accept the confusion and disorientation and allow the old self to die. This also means that one has to allow the new self to be born—a natural process. This inner stance becomes even more challenging when friends, family, and colleagues negate and actively oppose this major transformation in lifestyle and values. Trusting in the wisdom of one's soul, in the psycho-spiritual process, and in a different worldview are the ways that a seeker is able to successfully get through these challenges.

Expanding consciousness through Breathwork, meditation, and/or dream analysis in combination with individual psycho-spiritual counseling and guidance, as described in chapter one, can also be very helpful during this time. Such support will help to strengthen the awareness on how to integrate heightened spiritual consciousness into daily life.

Kinds of Psycho-Spiritual Work: Two Examples

The following examples describe Jonas and Kay, two clients whose stories demonstrate how their psycho-spiritual process evolved:

Jonas

Jonas is a 35 year-old computer analyst who came to see me shortly after his divorce and subsequent DUI. I originally believed that his anger and depression reflected the hurt he was feeling after 15 years of a marriage gone awry. A traditional psychological intervention would have been to address

Jonas' "presenting problem," which was to learn how to keep his anger and drinking under control. The course of our work together changed, however, when I asked him whether he ever wondered about his purpose in life, about God, and what his current unhappiness meant for his personal development. Jonas replied that he had no religion and rejected the idea that there was meaning in any of the events in his life. He stressed that he believed that everything that occurs in life is random—and that he, in this case, was merely a victim.

I recall responding that I could understand his gloom and anger if he had no faith or even hope for what happens in the world and in his life. Yet the "Big Questions" that I asked opened a surprising and very different sort of conversation concerning something that Jonas had kept private since childhood. He told me that since about age nine, he had been hearing voices. Most of the voices, he said, were helpful. Others tried to discourage him and affirmed his feelings of hopelessness about life. He admitted that he had been to therapy before, both as a child and as an adult, but he had never discussed the voices with a therapist because "most people hear them, don't they?"

I told Jonas that, in fact, most people do not hear inner voices. Because he did, I asked him whether living at this level of consciousness was causing confusion for him. My question to Jonas came from my experience of working with other people who also hear voices and are very troubled by them. I said to him, "I imagine what it must be like to hear voices in your head at the same time you are speaking to another person, or trying to pay attention to your environment." Therefore, I was surprised at

Jonas' response. Since these voices had been with Jonas since he was a young boy, he basically accepted them and dealt with them in a very mature manner.

"How do you make sense of what you hear?" I asked

"I think they come from the good and bad parts of me," he answered.

I supported Jonas in his belief and told him that they were there for healing, trying to show him his true nature, because he was having difficulty finding peace and clarity about his life. And when the negative voices came, I suggested that they might be a reflection of his fears, early trauma, unresolved questions, and the emotional chaos that he experienced in his childhood and adult years.

As we worked together, Jonas became more clear as to which voices came from his authentic Self and which from his fears. He eventually learned how to identify the factors that had disconnected him from his emotions and intuition—he had learned early on to bury his pain and had been rewarded by his macho father and emotionally-suppressed mother for doing so.

Shortly after Jonas began Breathwork and psycho-spiritual work with me, the voices that had been with him for most of his life began to disappear. As he learned to access and trust his soul's wisdom, he no longer needed voices—good or bad—to tell him how to feel and behave.

Kay

Kay was fifty when I met her, and she had been in therapy most of her adult life. She told me that all of those years and thousands of dollars she had spent had never helped her resolve a tremendous sense of loss and lack of fulfillment. She had been a musical prodigy as a child, but as an adult could not find the joy she had once known in self-expression. She frequently saw doctors for a wide range of complaints including depression and chronic pain.

Kay grew up with a mother who rejected her and a father who sexually abused her. She had a few friends in school, but her only real pleasure, the only place where she felt nurtured and truly herself was in her music. Her piano teacher and others had recognized Kay's talent and she attended a prestigious conservatory. Yet decades later, she had not realized her potential.

Why was Kay unable to express her musical gift? What kind of psychotherapy had she had? How had it failed her for nearly half of her lifetime?

I learned more about the devastating effects of Kay's sexual and emotional abuse when I read what she wrote about her sled "accident" at age seven. It soon became apparent that the incident she referred to was, in fact, intentional. She had attempted to commit suicide by running her sled into a cement bench. At the moment of impact, she had a Near-Death Experience (NDE). She reports that she saw a brilliant white light that protected her from harm and heard the words:

"You have made a mistake. Your life is not yours to throw away. You will go back and take care of your body and discover who you are. Then you will open, and open even more, and have your own family with children you will love and nurture."

Kay did grow up, marry, and raise a family of three happy and successful children. Her achievement was a testament to her loving nature, but still she suffered. She told me that she believed in the Light that had saved her years before, but she thought it had come from an outside source and she did not know how to access it again. She did not understand that the light she spoke about was also within her, and that it could in fact help reignite her creative self.

Despite the fact that both parents had been dead for years, Kay was still angry at her mother's coldness and felt ashamed and violated by her father's abuse. This inner darkness was thwarting her soul's longing for expression and manifesting in psychosomatic symptoms.

When Kay recounted her therapeutic history, I learned she had made two serious attempts at psychotherapy after she left home. The first time was with a Dr. S., who through talk therapy had tried to help her gain insight into her early childhood abuse so that she could rationally decide to let go of the negative emotions and move on.

After a rational approach was unable to free Kay from her depression, she chose a therapist who wanted to help her express all the anger, shame, and pain she had felt over the years. In spite of this, her sense of emptiness remained.

Unfortunately, neither of Kay's therapists was willing to discuss or help her access the Light that had come to her so many years before. Spirituality was never discussed. Thus, she was left without a source of inner strength or an ability to create out of her true nature.

Kay's failed experiences of psychotherapy suggest that there is something that mental health practitioners don't see. After a client's "psychopathology" is identified and begins to go away, many therapists end treatment, believing that the individual has been "cleaned out" and cured. Instead, clients are left feeling a void, still disconnected from their source of inner strength. If instead they learned to acknowledge and invoke this part of themselves, they would feel alive and energized instead of lonely and disoriented.

The voice, light and vision that Kay had experienced in her childhood NDE had a profound impact on her life. As I have said, mystical experiences reveal the deepest truths about our nature, and nothing that occurs in traditional psychotherapy is comparable. Rather than stigmatizing her inner messages as signs of mental illness, I let Kay know that I respected her visionary experiences, and believed that they had occurred for the purpose of her healing. She began doing Breathwork sessions with me so that she could learn through the practice of expanding her consciousness that the healing source she had experienced as a child would still be there when she opened to it.

Ultimately, Kay had three visions during Breathwork that provided her with the most help. The first was of an eagle, a bird that in many traditions around the world symbolizes the spiritual light of the sun, heaven, and divine omnipotence. This validated Kay's early experience of light and her long search to find it again. The second vision was of herself as a Viking, which led her to research her ancestral roots on the Isle of Man, an island off the coast of England. There, she reconnected with her Celtic identity when she met two of her cousins for the first time and joyfully sang with them in an ancient Celtic musical and poetry festivity.

Kay's third breakthrough happened with a mystical vision of Christ on the cross. In the same moment, she experienced his essential message of forgiveness. Her heart opened wide, and she suddenly felt love, compassion, and reconciliation with her parents.

Being able to forgive brought a new freedom into Kay's life. She is no longer plagued by frequent illnesses and now is in the process of writing and performing her own musical compositions. By dissolving the darkness of her past through connecting with her inner light, she also renewed the connection with her creative source.

CHAPTER 8

STAGE TWO: ILLUMINATION

*The intrinsic core, the essence, the universal nucleus
of every known high religion...has been the private,
lonely, personal illumination, revelation, or ecstasy
of some acutely sensitive prophet or seer."*

—Abraham Maslow (1970)

A 45-year-old woman named Ellen came to see me because she
had been having disturbing nightmares almost every night for
several months. She dreaded going to sleep and spent each day
anxious and exhausted. I had known her slightly for approximately ten years as a neighbor and an interested member of the
community. I also knew that she was divorced, a single mother,
and had been a first grade teacher for twenty years.

Ellen told me that in her dreams she was always taken
back to her childhood home, where she observed the repeated
sexual and emotional abuse she had suffered for many years
from her brother, her uncle, and even her own mother. As she
shared the details and acknowledged that what she witnessed
in her nightmares was, in fact, all true, I was quite taken

aback. I wondered how she could have endured such a tortu-
ous past and now appear so kind, personable, and emotionally
high-functioning. She had raised a fine son who, as a teenager,
is a model young man and student. She is also active socially
and politically in the community and has many good friends
and close neighbors. Her horrific history did not seem to fit the
Ellen I knew.

As she and I continued to meet, I discovered that she had
a deep spiritual nature, although she did not use spiritual ter-
minology in her interactions with people, nor was she affiliated with any church, synagogue, or New Age group. I learned
that God was the center of Ellen's life. She told me that she felt
connected to a "sacred force," and it is this force to which she
has dedicated her life. Mystical experiences have abounded for
many years—visions of brilliant light, of Jesus, and a sense of His
love and support. There have also been visions of other religious
deities and the sense of a close connection with angels, Hindu
goddesses, and with Buddha as well.

Despite her recent challenges, Ellen told me that she trusts
that her God connection is always present. "For some reason,"
she said, "I need to suffer right now and I don't understand why.
I do have faith and trust in my spiritual process, and I've always
believed that God healed me from my early abuse and trauma,
so why is all this evil coming around again to haunt me?"

Our real work together initiated from this question. I
responded by telling her that I believed she was currently functioning in "Illumination," the second stage of the Western spiritual path. "There are two major characteristics of this stage," I

said, "and you have been living through the first for many years. Now, you are beginning to deal with the second."

Characteristics of Spiritual Illumination

The hallmark of this stage, unlike in the first stage, is an increase in the number of mystical experiences, very similar to those Ellen described, such as the visions of light, Jesus, and other deities. The second, which was just beginning to come to expression through dreams, is the natural process of purification, manifested in an increased upsurge of unresolved psycho-emotional issues that need to be healed in order to restore the person to their authentic nature.

1. Mystical Experiences: The First Characteristic

I realized that Ellen was in the second stage because it was clear that her spiritual life encompassed much more than an occasional glimpse of the transcendent, as is typical in stage one. At her core, she clearly already felt connected to God. As I shared in the chapter on our mystical roots, Western mysticism describes this deep center as "something indestructible in the depths that never gives way," or "the Kingdom of God within."[96]

Before the nightmares began, Ellen had been living her life with an intense degree of vitality, a more acute degree of perception, with experiences that pointed to a more vivid consciousness than most people sustain. The monk and poet Gerard Manley Hopkins (1844-1889) described it well: "The world is charged with the grandeur of God." [97] It seemed that Ellen had continual communication with the Divine, which is typical in this stage, and these experiences brought joy and fulfillment. In such a state of consciousness, dreams provide guidance, everyday life feels imbued with sacredness, and existential loneliness disappears. Rather than causing a transient ecstatic high, Stage Two experiences now feel like part of life, eliciting faith, trust, and awe.

As a result of the continual shedding of ego and working with the shadow in Awakening, seekers in Stage Two have come to slowly but surely identify with another order of reality. Consciousness shifts from being self-centered to God-centered, and this God-centered reality is not a metaphor, but a certainty felt as sharply as the other senses. Thus, the consciousness of Illumination is an organic evolution of the process initiated in Stage One.

With such a spiritually profound inner life, what more could there be? In fact, this stage is only a halfway mark on the path. Western mystics consider it the betrothal rather than the marriage of the soul. Why? Because there is still a separation between the seeker and the Divine. "This is still not God; rather, it is the light in which we see Him," wrote the great Christian mystic John of Ruysbroeck (1293–1381)."[98] In other words, the seeker is not yet immersed "in God," but experiences the divine as something "witnessed," rather than deeply known by the individual self.

2. Increased Light, Increased Darkness: The Second Characteristic

The experience of Light in the individual is the same as the God Light in all things. However, its manifestation is subject to the influences of one's past, temperament, environment, and heredity. In its most positive expression, it will amplify one's personality and special gifts—this is what many of Ellen's friends, colleagues, and acquaintances experienced when they were around her. More than one called her "a shining light."

As Ellen became more connected to her inner light and the process of healing, powerful spiritual energy continued to push deep and still-unresolved shadow came up into awareness, causing times of emotional stress. This is why, although her spiritual connection was very meaningful, and had in fact brought her much healing, I did not think it was enough.

She was shocked by my words: "What else is there?" she asked. "God is everything and all there is…what else can there be?"

"There is," I told her gently, "the necessity for you to reexamine your childhood abuse and the effects it has had on your personality and life."

"But I've gotten over it," she said, puzzled, "I've forgiven my family and put it away."

"Ellen," I said, "You would not be having continual nightmares if everything has been resolved. There is also your divorce of ten years ago. Why have you not gone out with any other men since?"

"It is true that you have spiritually grown and created a positive life for yourself and your son. But the effects of abuse are still buried deep in you. It is probably why you married an abuser and have not looked for a different partner to love in your life. Even if you are not conscious of these thoughts and feelings, they are still alive in you. Your dreams are relentlessly pushing you to face your early trauma once again, this time in order to bring about greater healing and resolution."

My response to Ellen is another example of why I call such work psycho-spiritual. Even though Ellen is in the second stage of the path, there is still very deep emotional trauma in her soul that is trying to heal. My training as a psychologist was important at this stage of her journey.

Ellen slowly began to understand my words as we continued to work together. And in time she came to appreciate the teaching her nightmares brought to her. Through Breathwork she once again experienced the agony of her abuse, but this time, unlike in her nightmares, spiritual light also came up and began to dissolve the darkness, her heart opened, and she felt love take away the residual remnants of pain.

In the process of going through Spiritual Illumination, discordant elements of the personality are literally illuminated in order to bring greater self-knowledge. In Ellen's case, it helped her to become aware of ways that her experience of abuse was still holding her back, not only from a relationship with a man, but from progressing to the final stage of Union.

I also call the second characteristic of Illumination a "Shift to the Inner Teacher." Seekers learn to trust the guidance coming through their soul—often in dreams and intuition. In the words of the poet William Blake (1757–1827), "the doors of perception are cleansed, so that everything appears infinite."[99] The messages coming to Ellen through her nightmares, however, were neither understood nor appreciated and, in fact, made her deeply upset.

She recognized she was blocked and needed help.

As Ellen and I continued to work together, she gradually became aware, even while dealing with issues of past trauma, that there was spiritual support and wisdom always available to her in her deepest core self. At last, she met her inner teacher, described by Ken Wilber as the great I AM. Three years since we worked together, the nightmares are long gone, she lives fulfilled in a deep spiritual process, and is happily remarried to a very loving man.

Jewish and Christian Perspectives about Illumination

Illumination is a time of major spiritual growth and development. Unlike in Stage One, the sense of a Divine Presence no longer feels like a temporary high, but rather is an ongoing, nurturing reality that is always available. The more a seeker recognizes the power of God consciousness, the more important it becomes to continue to heal the soul and self-knowledge becomes paramount. As the connection to this inner wisdom strengthens, there is the sense of ordered activity within, but with a core of stillness. The Augustinian mystic Walter Hilton (c. 1396) called this inner state, "A rest most busy."[100] Reverend Abraham Isaac Kook, a mystic and chief rabbi of Palestine (1922), referred to Illumination as "a thirst for the living God," in that all desire is directed towards an immediate, rather than an abstract, experience of the divine.[101] The Catholic nun Hildegard of Bingen (1098–1179), who had visions throughout her life beginning from the age of three, described this state as an experience of "so great a special light, more brilliant than the brightness round the sun."[102]

In Illumination, the soul can no longer be satisfied with mere reflections of that Light in this world; even morality and goodness are not enough, nor do the deep truths in books or exalted forms of beauty satisfy.

Wrote Kook:

> "Now, from our own depths, the truth discloses itself to us: All things that exist draw their light from the most sublime source. Every dimension of being, every creation is a revelation of the infinite Light. Throughout our lives, these creations have appeared to us in fragmentary ways, as sparks of light. But now we grasp their true essence, we know they are parts of a single organism, a single revelation embracing all beauty, all illumination, all truth and all goodness." [103]

Both Jewish and Christian mystics of the past described the deep joy in the state of Illumination, even while the journey continued to bring more challenges, both in work with the shadow and also in terms of staying committed and in surrender to the process.

Challenges of Spiritual Illumination

Given that Illumination represents a mature level of spiritual development, it is not surprising that there would be numerous inherent challenges for seekers as they attempt to live out of this stage of consciousness. There are five key challenges encountered in Stage Two. These are: 1) feelings of grandiosity; 2) being overwhelmed; 3) the experience of the "dark night of the soul;" 4) the challenge of staying connected to one's spiritual process; and 5) premature states of Union.

1. Grandiosity

In the early stages of Illumination, it is all too easy to assume that spiritual and mystical experiences are the primary goal. Thus, rather than focusing on dealing with one's inner shadow, a person's ego gets caught up in this new reality and one feels special and uniquely chosen by God. If the seeker is charismatic, other seekers may become attracted by his or her personality and become students, and sometimes even disciples. The result, dependency and adulation (usually from those in Awakening), contribute to a state of ego glorification and personal power. Without a continuing commitment to work with the shadow, the stage two seeker will become spiritually stuck and unable to move forward. Stories of spiritual groups or communities where the teacher or guru has been trapped in his or her ego are all too common and lead to exploitation and even abuse of those who are students. This happens both in the West and in the East. The tragedy of the self-styled preacher Jim Jones and the group suicide of his followers, for example, and the many claims of exploitation and sexual abuse from the students of the Indian guru Sai Baba.[104]

While much less dramatic than either Jim Jones or Sai

Baba, the following story is an example of what can occur when a well-intentioned contemporary spiritual guide identifies at the ego level with her spiritual process:

Terry

Terry was a body worker with a considerable background in metaphysics. A personable woman in her thirties, she had attended numerous New Age workshops and when I met her she was providing "spiritual healing" to her clients. Having had numerous Stage two experiences, she considered herself very spiritually evolved and psychologically aware. She came to see me because she had been feeling bored and frustrated for some months, despite her many friends, successful career, and a fine relationship with a man who shared an interest in her work.

During our first session, Terry told me that she felt as if her world was falling apart. She had been feeling depressed, angry, losing interest in her chosen profession, and felt at a loss to come up with an explanation for her discontent.

When I asked Terry about her worldview, she quickly responded that she had a deep understanding of spirituality, had been helping her clients through doing energy healing, had participated in many workshops herself, and had been giving presentations and demonstrations to groups.

I pressed her further, asking, "How have you worked with your inner shadow and light?"

"Well, spirituality has been my work and my life," Terry responded, starting to look confused, perhaps wondering whether I was not very intelligent, and perhaps beginning to think that I did not understand how spiritually advanced she truly was. "Do you feel like you have a relationship with a Higher Power, with God?" I asked her.

Terry was stunned into silence, unable to respond to either of my questions. It became clear that she was not really sure how she felt about God and felt more comfortable "owning" spiritual power than realizing it did not belong to her.

Today, Terry has temporarily set her healing practice aside and is now working as a receptionist in a lawyer's office while she engages in psycho-spiritual work. She and I are looking at her ego issues and her ambivalence about the nature of God. She has realized that her early family dynamics caused her to distrust the idea of a spiritual force beyond herself. Her father abandoned the family when she was a young child; therefore, she believed there was no one whom she could trust, not even a Higher Power. In order to earn her father's love and attention, she had grown up believing that she had to accomplish "great" things. Becoming a highly recognized healer was therefore gratifying at many levels.

Although Terry still has occasional feelings of depression and even emptiness, she is trying to open to a spiritual reality that is within and also beyond—much more than her. She continues to explore the dysfunction in her early family life, realizing that in order to help heal others, she must first heal her own issues. She looks forward to a time when she will have gained a level of spiritual and psychological strength that she can authentically share with others.

When I work with individuals stuck in grandiosity, I always

encourage them to see that what comes through their soul has nothing to do with personal identity or power. Rather, they need to recognize that they are the channels through which sacred energy expresses itself. Only with such humility will they be able to successfully travel their path and assist others on the spiritual journey.

2. Being Overwhelmed

Another Stage Two challenge manifests when the intensity of Illuminative experience becomes overwhelming. Jack's story is an example. A sensitive artist who always felt drawn to metaphysical, philosophical, and spiritual topics, his paintings reflect his deep quest, and I have several of them hanging in my home. I had known Jack for quite a few years and was impressed by his quiet, laid-back demeanor. I was quite surprised, therefore, when he called me for an appointment and began speaking in a very disorganized and agitated state.

During our first session, Jack told me that for most of his life he had felt drawn to spiritual questions because of an abiding sense that he had contact with a consciousness much greater than his own. While he stayed away from organized religion, he trusted his own connection and believed that this expressed itself through his abstract paintings.

All was well in Jack's life until visions, voices, and synchronicities suddenly and inexplicably began to occur, so intense and frequent that he felt pulled into a vortex and his sense of a separate identity and self seemed all but annihilated. There were also visions of fire, crucifixion, and resurrection. This was particularly perplexing because Jack had not attended church for his entire adult life and his parochial Catholic schooling had ended many decades ago.

After we worked together for a while, Jack began to realize that there was something incomplete for him in his spiritual process. As it turned out, although he had decided when he reached adulthood that he no longer wanted anything to do with Catholicism, he had unknowingly rejected certain aspects of his religious heritage that were not only authentic, but still vitally present in his soul. He had legitimate reason to complain about a lack of soul nourishment in the particular church he attended in his youth but, in so doing, he also unwittingly rejected a deep part of his own spiritual identity and inner truth.

Through our work together, Jack began to accept and commit to his Western mystical heritage that was suddenly and unexpectedly coming through him in his visions and intensely spiritual feelings. This was the breakthrough that needed to happen. Because Jack was able to put his ego aside and accept that his current mystical experiences and visions had nothing to do with his childhood church, his life and art were transformed.

3. Dark Night of the Soul

Of all of the challenges on the path, perhaps the best known is the experience of the "Dark Night of the Soul," described by mystics and saints across the ages.[105] Contemporary spiritual teachers and religious scholars in the West, including the bestselling author Thomas Moore, have also written about this passage.[106] It is, in fact, becoming a common reference and I have observed that many spiritually-inclined seekers claim mistakenly that they are experiencing a "dark night of the soul" during such times when they are depressed, disappointed about issues like the loss of a job, a problem at work, or a love relationship gone awry.

The Dark Night of the Soul has little to do with the challenges of daily life. The true meaning has to do with one's relationship with God. It is often one of the final tests on the path. In fact, Dark Night is not so much a state of inner darkness as it is of utter emptiness, a spiritual void. Its main characteristic is that all spiritual experiences seem to stop. It is as if God has abandoned the seeker, and faith and the personal spiritual connection are eradicated without possibility of recovery. There is no longer anything to orient to, neither worldly ego gratification (since there has been ego loss), nor spiritual fulfillment from Illuminative experiences. It is a helpless, desperate state.

The Jesuit Jean Pierre DeCaussade said when this total privation or "mystic death" is fully established, it involves not only the personal absence of God, but also the withdrawal of the transcendent ground on which the self has long believed its whole real life to be based."[107] St. John of the Cross called Dark Night a "passive purification," a state of helpless misery, in which the Self does nothing, but "lets life have its way with him." [108]

In Dark Night, it seems impossible to find the Light in the midst of such pain and suffering, yet the saying, "You have to be lost in order to be found," is relevant here. In fact, this painful state is yet another way for the Self to be purified. As in ego death, when the senses are cleansed and humbled, so now the purifying process is extended to the very center of personhood. An attachment to the spiritual ego and the sense of a special relationship with God is completely disrupted. This is a "spiritual crucifixion," the great desolation in which the soul seems abandoned by the Divine, in the sense of the words spoken by Jesus on the cross: "My God, my God, why hast Thou forsaken me?"[109] Moore describes this phenomenon in this way:

> When it comes to spiritual growth, we humans are solar-seeking beings; eager for the bright lights of clarity and the bliss of illumination. Unlike depression, which is more of an emotional state, the Dark Night is a slow transformation process, which is fueled by a profound period of doubt, disorientation and questioning. Paradoxically, we all need to walk through the shadow of the Dark Night in order to discover a life worth living.[110]

Frances, a longtime meditator, kept many journals over the years in which she recorded her most significant spiritual experiences. She was successfully leading meditation workshops, believing that she had completed her spiritual path. She came to me devastated after she suddenly began experiencing what she called a spiritual void, an inner emptiness that felt like death. Not only did her meditation practice become inconsequential, she no longer felt that she had anything to offer her students.

In some ways, Frances's story is similar to that of Terry earlier in this chapter. Terry became a spiritual teacher without ever having an authentic connection with God. Frances had had many experiences of God, but as I pointed out to her over the months that we worked together, spiritual development means to lose enough ego so that one realizes that one is but an empty vessel through which God energy passes. I explained that she was in Dark Night of the Soul and showed her ways in which her ego was attached to her spiritual experiences. I explained why any attachment, even in the spiritual realm, must be released in order to reach the final stage of Union.

4) Attempts to Control and Edit One's Spiritual Process

As I have said earlier, I have regularly witnessed spiritual seekers—Christian, Jewish, agnostic, Buddhists, practitioners of shamanism—unexpectedly have very strong experiences related to our Western spiritual heritage during Breathwork, and at other times as well. Like Jack, the artist who initially rejected his Catholic mystical heritage, many people are stunned, bewildered, and become disoriented and resistant when spiritual experiences come that they don't want or don't expect. A particularly difficult issue concerns mystical experiences of Jesus, especially if the person has rejected one of the forms of Western organized religion.

This is the point where my work becomes very challenging. As I've said in earlier chapters, the primary message I share with clients is to open to and accept whatever comes through their spiritual process, whether in dreams, meditation, prayer, Breathwork, or everyday life. Whatever the image, symbol, or spiritual energy, it is unique for the individual and has specific meaning and purpose for their lives and spiritual development.

This is true whether the vision is of a shamanic power animal, the Hindu elephant God Ganesh, their own personal guardian angel, Jesus, or any other kind of energy.

When people are able to open to whatever spiritual experience comes, letting go of resistances and attempts to control their process, spiritual development speeds up immensely.

5) Blocks to the Final Stage of Union

As seekers progress through the stages, premature states of Union, the final stage of the path, sometimes begin to manifest. Such events can occur early as part of the first stage of Awakening and also be common in Illumination. Yet no matter how blissful or ecstatic this may seem, I remind people that their journey is primarily about purification and healing. Only when ego and unresolved shadow is dissolved will it be possible to truly live in the stage of being one with All.

A Longing for Union Blocked by a Co-dependent Relationship

The following two stories exemplify the sorts of emotional issues and confusion that can occur when a state of Union is experienced, but the seeker is not yet prepared to fully integrate it.

Fay's story is the opposite of my student Mark's experience of Union, which he had while heading home on the subway. He was disoriented after losing the sense of a boundary between himself and others, especially because he had never before had a spiritual experience of any kind. Fay, however, had reached a point in her spiritual development where Union was possible. But she became blocked from fully merging with God because she had merged with her husband instead. Psychology typically uses the term "co-dependency" in such cases, to refer to someone who has lost a sense of self because of an unhealthy emotional attachment to another. Fay was 52, very sensitive, spiritually aware and had worked hard in therapy and in Breathwork for many years. When she began to experience strong states of Union, she became filled with anxiety and was unable to integrate those experiences, because she realized at some level, it meant that she would have to open up to living differently, with the knowledge of God in every aspect of her life. Through committed inner work, she eventually understood that she was in a co-dependent relationship with her husband, a man who had a scientific worldview. In certain subtle ways, his identity and worldview had become her own. Unable to break out of this pattern, she chose to stay merged with the relationship. This meant that she was unable to access the divine in the core of her being, because her husband lived there instead.

As I have said, the closer a person comes to the final stage, the more the remnants of the shadow self will become evident. Illumination and Union are about connection and Oneness. Therefore, the shadow material that comes up often can reflect separation and division. This is what happened with Irene in the following story.

A Longing for Union Blocked by Fear of Intimacy

Irene was a supervisor in a women's counseling center. She came to me with the admission that she had difficulty maintaining close relationships with people. After experiencing a powerful state of Union in a Breath workshop, her fears of intimacy disappeared as her heart opened. She began to feel particularly close and loving towards the people in her life and told me that her previous feelings of separation, especially those created by the hierarchy between herself and her supervisees, and between herself and her family members, suddenly felt all but non-existent.

Irene felt blissful and grounded for about a month. Then she began to talk about feeling stifled by her partner, Bruce. Many of her past romantic relationships had been characterized by an "approach-avoidance" tendency—a need for intimacy followed the desire for space and distance once the need was met. This duality reflects a deep inner conflict, which often becomes exacerbated after an experience of Union, because the contrast between being separate, versus feeling open, emotionally close, and One with other people can be very strong. Thus, although Irene's heart had been open, she closed it to Bruce, and pulled away because, as she admitted to me, she was afraid that she would lose herself. In her psycho-spiritual work, she had to spend time facing those fears and strengthening her connection to her inner Light before she could progress.

Longing for Union Blocked by Fear of Losing One's Identity

The fear of losing one's identity is the biggest hindrance of all, because when all is said and done, most of us like to think that we are somebody. To give up being *somebody* in order to become *nobody* is very difficult in Western culture, with its emphasis on independence and personal achievement. Yet in Illumination, we are being prepared to lose our ego and any sense that we live apart from God.

In Spiritual Illumination, we come to realize that the light coming through our soul is not for us alone. Rather, it is to be expressed in the world for the benefit of others. As such, personal ambition, or holding on to the illusion that we "own" our spiritual power cannot sustain. In preparation for the final stage of Union, seekers gradually come to realize that their self is becoming an empty container in which personal identity and ego are rapidly disappearing. This open space provides the inner expansiveness where God energy can live and grow in preparation for serving the greater good.

Resolving and Integrating Spiritual Illumination

Even in the heightened process of Illumination, people feel challenged. Living in our untransformed world with an Illuminated consciousness becomes an ongoing struggle in the soul. Those who successfully move through to Union find ways to come to terms with this challenge.

As I have said, when desire, ego, and feelings of needing to be in control are surrendered, then and only then is the seeker ready to become One with the Divine. The lessons, therefore, of this stage, can be best summarized by the words acceptance, surrender, and faith. How long the challenges last depends on how long it takes to let go of the perception that one is separate and distinct from anyone else or from God.

A Modern Seeker's Thoughts about the Western Spiritual Path

David was a Jesuit brother and doctoral student at Columbia University. A man in his late thirties, he has been on the path for many years, experiencing over and over a state of either ego loss or spiritual illumination. "The closer I move toward the light, the more the shadows are revealed," said David. "It has been so hard and devastating that I have been tempted to give it all up completely."

David's description of his journey underscores my earlier comment that the path is not a series of methodical steps leading upward, but more of a spiral. "It was in the fall of my senior year in college," David wrote in an email to me, "that I had an experience in prayer that confirmed not only how real God is, but that I needed to take my relationship with God as the point of departure for whatever life choices I made from there on. The experience filled me with joy and fear, gratitude and sadness, and that profound sense of ambivalent nature of the encounter with God—a dialectical tension between attraction lived out in religious life as a Jesuit and dread of this relationship because of the cost to my ego."

David says he has been fortunate to meet "very good guides and companions along the way--spiritual directors, saints, and poets as well." Today he is grounded in the visionary spirituality of the Jesuits while also practicing Centering Prayer, which he calls "a spiritual practice that emphasizes more of an emptiness and continual letting go."

He added that he had moved on from Zen back to the Western Christian practice of Centering that stems from the Benedictine tradition because, while similar to Zen, it includes the "I/ Thou" relationship with the Divine (immanently manifest and transcendent).

I have known many traveling the Western Spiritual Path say that, despite the challenges, it is what makes life worth living. Throughout the wonders and shadow trials of Illumination, they hold onto their faith as they anticipate fulfillment. As Evelyn Underhill so wisely wrote, "Enlightenment is a symptom of growth: and growth is a living process, which knows no rest."

As you will see in the next chapter, the living process does bear fruit at last.

CHAPTER 9

STAGE THREE: UNION

When you train yourself to hear the voice of God in everything, you attain the quintessence of the human spirit.

—Rabbi Abraham Isaac Kook (1865–1935)

Jesus said to them: When you make the two one, and when you make the inner as the outer; and the outer as the inner and the above as the below, and when you make the male and female into a single one… then shall you enter the Kingdom.

—The Gnostic Gospel of St. Thomas (First Century C.E.)

Union: the final stage

Personal ego dramas and worn-out life stories have fallen away and lost their significance. The individual soul and God are one. God is the only reality, the way life is lived, and the heart's deep truth. Now, there is the experience of "simply being," wholly in the present moment. Now, there is new energy, enthusiasm, and life is Sacredness. This stage is our birthright and the true culmination of a life well lived.

Chief Black Elk of the Oglala Sioux Nation (1863–1950) is reported to have said, "The first peace, which is the most important, is that which comes within the souls of people when they realize their relationship, their Oneness, with the universe and all its powers, and when they realize that at the center of the universe dwells the Great Spirit, and that this center is really everywhere, it is within each of us."[111]

In the Qu'ran, the holy book of Islam, it is written, "The entire universe, in the way it is created, in the way it is controlled, bears witness to the Union or Oneness with Allah. And behind the forms is the One who gives them shape."[112] In the Mundaka Upanishad in Hinduism, we read: "Above time all is Brahman, One and Infinite. He is beyond north and south, east and west, above or below. *To the unity of that One goes he who knows this* [my emphasis]."[113]

Having an open heart, said the Jewish mystics, and knowing that we are not separate from God, are one and the same. "God is the stronghold of my heart" is a line in the 73rd psalm, a song of praise in the Old Testament.[114] With an open heart, we become like the Divine One, the inner space where all beings thrive.[115]

Union is known as "Luminosity-Emptiness" in Tibetan Buddhism: infinite, light-filled space. What better description of inner peace! Mind, heart and soul, empty of stress, worry, and meaningless chatter—and at the same time "full."

Become *Ayin* to Live in God

The Hasidic rabbi known as the Maggid of Mezritch (1704–1772) said that in order for one thing to be transformed into another, it must first come to *ayin*, a Hebrew word for Nothingness. "Think of yourself as *ayin*," he told his disciples, "and forget yourself totally. Then you can transcend time, rising to the world of thought, where all is equal: life and death, ocean and dry land. This is not the case when you are attached to the material nature of the world. If you think of yourself as *yesh*, as something, God cannot be clothed in you, for God is infinite, and no vessel can contain God—unless you think of yourself as *ayin*."[116]

This same teaching appears in the words of the Christian mystic St. John of the Cross (1542–1591):

To reach satisfaction in all,
desire its possession in nothing.

To come to possess all,
desire the possession of nothing.

To arrive at being all,
desire to be nothing.

To come to the knowledge of all,
desire the knowledge of nothing. [117]

Experiencing Union as Ayin: A Meditation by Estelle Frankel

The Maggid of Mezritch also taught that when we pray or meditate, we should contemplate our souls already merged with God, even though that stage might not yet be attained. The following meditation by psychotherapist Estelle Frankel is a practice for experiencing the separate self dissolving into nothingness:

- Imagine that you enter into the pause between breaths or the gap between thoughts.

- In that space you can begin to experience *ayin*, the divine emptiness that is the backdrop of all creation.

- Now come back to your body and notice that you are made up of the same cosmic stardust from which all creation was made. Everything that is out there is also within you.

- As you come to this realization, the boundaries between inside and outside begin to dissolve, and you can begin to experience the unity of all being within the divine.

- Let your soul dissolve into the Divine Presence like a raindrop falling into the sea or a wave breaking at the shore.

- Allow yourself to rest in *ayin* for as long as you are comfortable.

- When you are ready, become aware once more of your breath.

- Notice the boundaries of your body and your breath.

- Begin to notice where your body touches the surfaces beneath and around you.

- Become aware of your presence in space and time.

- You may wish to give your body a rubdown in order to reconnect with your physical boundaries before you gently open your eyes.[118]

Psychology's Problem with Union

Unlike a premature *state* of Union, the *stage* of Union is the culmination of our path. The perseverance, the shadow work, the
release of attachment to ego and a separate self, even the descent
into the void of Dark Night of the Soul all come together at last in
a state of balance and harmony. It is crucial that psychotherapists
recognize that such states of consciousness are of a wholly different order than psychological dependencies and fears. The field
of psychology, however, will often interpret a desire for the experience of Union as either a primitive need to return to the womb,
a sexual drive, or as psychosis. Specifically, this is exemplified in
some common principles of psychotherapy that mental health
professionals communicate to clients such as the importance
of maintaining strong personal boundaries and differentiation
between yourself and another and being aware of the threat of
co-dependency and symbiotic relationships. It is also stressed
that the hierarchy and role differences that separate client and
therapist are upheld. When a psychotherapist encourages indi-
viduation, personal empowerment, and boundary building with
a client who has had experienced Union—especially a premature state of Union, the individual will be left confused and without support for integrating the experience.

Although this ultimate stage may sound like sainthood, it
is just as available to ordinary people as it is for those individuals who left their mark on the history of Western spirituality.
Hopefully, the stories told in this book exemplify this. Still, I am
often asked, is it really possible for a person to live feeling whole,

part of the All, at peace, every moment, day and night? To feel centered and connected to everything always? To never be overwhelmed by fear and suffering? Unlikely as it may sound, I know people in today's world who mostly experience life this way. This is how the Byzantine monk St. Symeon the New Theologian (949–1022 AD) affirmed this spiritual truth ten centuries ago:

> Do not say that it is impossible to receive the Spirit of God. Do not say that it is possible to be made whole without Him. Do not say that one can possess Him without knowing it. Do not say that God does not manifest Himself to man. Do not say that men cannot perceive the divine light, or that it is impossible in this age! Never is it found to be impossible, my friends. On the contrary, it is entirely possible when one desires it.[119]

Several years ago, I had a powerful experience of Union. I was sitting in a circle of people at a retreat center in the Black Forest in Germany. It was the last morning of a five-day Breathwork retreat and my German co-leader, Ingo, was passing around a wooden baton, inviting each of the twenty participants in turn to share thoughts and feelings about our time together. This was an exercise that we often used for closure, to ensure that the deep inner work experienced at the retreat was fully integrated.

The baton came to me as the last member of the circle. Ingo and I sometimes share our feelings with group members because of the deep, personal nature of our time together. Those who had spoken earlier had remarked that it was going to be difficult to go back to everyday life, after their intense experiences.

I always have a range of emotions when I am working in Germany—from feeling unconditional warmth and loving connection with the German participants, to my own brand of angst as a Jew about working with the descendants of Nazis. Working out these contradictory splits over the years has led me to very deep parts of myself.

As I began to share what I was feeling, a bolt of strong energy suddenly shot through me. In an instant, I was catapulted to a level of consciousness that felt vastly different from my normal consciousness. Somewhat shocked and feeling vulnerable, I nevertheless began to hesitantly speak out of that consciousness to the group. "I will not have trouble going back to America," I said, "because I feel that there is no other place than right here. And right now, here, no opposites or dualities exist—no good or evil, no male or female, no night or day, no past or future, no life or death, no Germans or Jews. The only thing that exists is this moment—and in this eternal moment, everything is possible, everything exists, and we are all connected in God."

This particular experience of Union affected me differently from my previous episodes. Previously, I could recall, appreciate, and conceptually understand what my states of Union were about. But after this experience my consciousness has changed dramatically, with the result that most of the time I feel what I felt that day, wherever I am and whatever I'm doing. No matter what personal or professional challenges I encounter, I am unable to venture too far from knowing that the present moment is all there is, has ever been, and will always be. I find that I hold onto life's travails more lightly, with less discomfort.

Can I honestly say that I am now living in the stage of Union? All I can really say is that within every stage, there are new levels to know and process. We can never be pure consciousness, or perfect, by any means, because our spirits are bounded by our physical bodies. Thus, there is never an end point. While I feel that today I live in the stage of Union in many ways, I also know very well that Socrates was right when he said, "The more I learn, the more I learn how little I know."[120]

Different Ways to Experience Union

My client Richard experiences Union in an impersonal way. God is a divine nothingness or a dark brilliance beyond all rational comprehension. There is a sense of peace, a lack of attachment to worldly things, and a feeling of Oneness. When he started to do Breathwork sessions with me, this 45-year-old man was already practicing meditation for at least two hours every day in addition to running his own small printing business. When I asked him what drew him to such a time-consuming and challenging spiritual practice, he answered simply that this was the way he could live with God.

When he described his meditations to me, I soon understood. "Almost always now," he said, "when I close my eyes, I begin rather quickly to lose the sense of having a body. Behind my closed eyes, darkness shifts to light, clear white light envelops me, and then there is a feeling of emptiness. I am this emptiness. There is nothing but the wide-open clear space, filled with light; I am this open space and light, there is nothing else. There is no

Richard. There is only joy, love, peace, stillness. I am everything and nothing at the same time."

When I ask Richard, whether he has any kind of personal relationship with God (as described in Chapter Four), he does not quite understand. In his experience, there is no I/Thou relationship that many of the Western mystics describe. Rather, his way of experiencing Union is through the Impersonal transcendent…through the emptiness, the clear space, the Void. He manifests this energy in his everyday life, working long hours to make up for his time in daily meditation. I have never seen him anxious or ungrounded; he does not ponder the future or ruminate about the past, but seems to live fully in the moment. He has a quiet humility, the expression in his eyes is joyful and sincere and his heart is open to all.

The other way to experience Union is through a consciousness that the mystics called "Deification," described by St. Paul as "I live, yet not I, but God in me.[121] By "deification," there is no arrogant claim to identification with God. Rather, that it is a transfusion of the self by God, an entrance upon a new order of life. Thus, personality is not lost, but made more real.

People fully centered in Union understand this perspective well. Unlike the spiritual seeker who may still be caught in ego attachment, the individual truly living in Union knows that our task as spiritual beings is to allow the self to be transformed through a mystical process—where we can hold the light and express that sacred energy in service to others.

This is what the Jewish mystics meant when they spoke of *tikkun*, which means "healing and restoration" in Hebrew. When the use of *tikkun* appears in popular culture today, it is often in connection with social responsibility, which is certainly important. But without the sacred as the core focus, the transformative power of *tikkun* is limited. The original intent affirms that we are co-creators with divine energy, which we may manifest through our thoughts and deeds. Thus, we accomplish *Tikkun Olam*— "repair the world"—by transcending such polarities as good and evil, male and female, spirit and matter, chaos and order—in other words, by living in wholeness, able to hold the opposites in an effortless synthesis and not be pulled in one direction or another.

Christ Consciousness: A Special Form of Union on the Western Path

I have worked with many seekers for whom Jesus has become an inner guide. This particular awareness, often called Christ Consciousness, is a common experience particular to those with a Western spiritual heritage.

In his remarkable book, *The Starseed Transmissions,* writer Ken Carey shares a vision of this consciousness. In the late 1970s, Carey was a postal worker and living a very simple life. One night, while lying half-asleep in bed, he slipped spontaneously into a state of heightened awareness that lasted 11 days and included voices and visions offering a new possibility for transforming Western culture. He transcribed the messages he received and in one excerpt he wrote:

> Outside of time and space, you are One with the Creator, the All that is, the Source. But when your

consciousness moves within the context of a manifest universe, you become the Son (Daughter), the
Christ. In essence, you are the relationship between
Spirit and Matter, the mediator, the bridge, the
means through which the Creator relates to
Creation. You are life as it relates to planet earth,
eternity as it relates to time, the infinite as it relates
to the finite. Though you presently experience
yourself as a separate and fragmented species, you
are in fact, a single unified being, sharing the consciousness of the Creator.[122]

The German mystic Meister Eckhart wrote similar words
600 years ago: "Though we are God's sons and daughters, we do
not realize it yet."[123]

The Western path is a process of transformation that makes
a human being another Christos, an awakened child of the
Creator. This process can be found in the story of the passion,
death, and resurrection of Jesus. But unlike much of mainstream
Christianity, the mystics taught that Jesus's story is not merely an
external act of salvation, but depicts the journey of the individual soul. Jesus's words, "The Kingdom of God is within," is the
call for inner transformation. His crucifixion mirrors the surrender of the ego. And His resurrection is a rebirth of the self,
transformed, awakened, and whole.

The Unique Challenge of Intimate and Personal Union with Jesus

If seekers are open to the experience of Jesus when he comes to them, I have observed how they progress more quickly on the spiritual path, eventually coming to trust that His love and divine energy is always available as a support in life. The nature and intensity of this relationship will usually go through different evolutions as the seeker's spiritual life matures. At a certain point, there is a profound shift that initially can be confusing, but which ultimately signifies the final stage. My client Rosemary is an example:

A 47-year-old attorney, Rosemary had been having visions of Jesus for many years during her Breathwork practice and during times of personal prayer. She would visualize and ask for His advice whenever she felt the need for guidance. When she felt conflicted, she told me during a session, her choices would be strongly influenced by what she understood that Jesus wanted her to do. Sometimes she would write questions in her journal, and usually an answer would come through her dreams. She sensed that these answers were evidence of Jesus's presence.

Rosemary did not grow up in a religious family; her devotion to Jesus came about because of her mystical experiences and because of the wisdom she said that He shared with her. She believed his continual spiritual guidance helped her to grow and transform her life.

I recall the evening that Rosemary came to our therapy session seemingly very upset. She told me that several weeks earlier

Jesus had suddenly disappeared from her world. She no longer saw Him when she closed her eyes, nor did she hear the gentle inner voice that she had grown to love so much. Then she said, with tears in her eyes, "Something really very strange happened and I don't know how to think about it."

Rosemary shared that during a meditation she had seen an image of Jesus as usual, and she became aware of her strong rush of familiar feelings of warmth, love, and gratitude towards him. Then, suddenly, His eyes seemed to become her eyes; His sacred heart became her heart; His body became united with hers; and then, He disappeared inside of her and became Her.

She told me that she felt abandoned and alone and she wanted to know how she could find that same connection again.

"Rosemary," I said gently. "It may take a while for you to trust what has changed in your relationship, but in fact, this is a very big shift that has taken place within you. The mystics called what you are experiencing 'Intimate and Personal Union with Jesus.' In essence, His consciousness is now merged with your own. Now, instead of only knowing Jesus as a loving guide and support outside of yourself, his energy has become your energy, available to shine through everything that you do in life."

Rosemary eventually let go of the separate connection and opened herself to this new and powerful awareness. Today she is still an attorney practicing family law. Modest and unassuming, her kindness, wisdom, and Christ Consciousness permeates everything she does. Her clients trust her intelligence, big heart and highly ethical nature. She considers herself a healer, not a litigator, and spends most of her time guiding people through the challenging process of divorce.

Even though Richard and Rosemary experience the Divine differently, the effects of integrating Union into their lives look remarkably similar. People feel calm and happy in their presence. As a friend of Rosemary's told her, "I feel like I want to be a better person when I am around you."

Christ Consciousness and the Power of Love, Compassion, and Forgiveness

The story of the life of Jesus emphasizes the significance of love between humanity and God. By surrendering his life to God, Jesus became transparent to that divine energy, which shone through his every word and deed. The 12th century monk Bernard of Clairvaux wrote: "The measure of love is to love beyond measure." We can only understand this message when we are released from the burden of our mental and emotional shadows. Today, it is so important for us to understand that society's institutions cannot erase darkness in individuals or in the world community. Opening the soul to divine energy is the only way. When Divine light, this love beyond measure flows, it immediately begins to heal and transform.

In his book *Son of Man: The Mystical Path to Christ*, contemporary mystic Andrew Harvey writes of his own experience of Christ Consciousness in the stage of Union:

> "Now in Union, lover, beloved, and love are all known as one; the Christ Consciousness is born

complete and the divine Child, radiant and eternal, appears at the core of awareness. All the powers of body, mind, heart, and soul are united in a fire of human divine love; the universe is experienced as a constant dance of supreme consciousness.... At last, the seeker enters into the "undivided" life of the Kingdom; the inner Christ that has been growing through all the ordeals and revelations of the journey now gazes consciously through the seeker's eyes, moves in the seeker's body, burns as divine love in all the cells of the seeker's heart."[124]

Harvey's poetic description of his own process is not unlike the writings of ancient sages and mystics. Christ Consciousness is universal, accessible and relevant for all of us.

It is challenging to let go of all fear and control, to lead a life that is God-directed rather than ego-directed. It requires trust, surrender, and motivation in order to successfully pass through each stage and integrate its energies into one's life. But in this third and final stage of Union, long-standing psychological dramas and personal stories are no longer relevant. The seeker knows beyond a shadow of a doubt that he or she is much more than a physical body with thoughts and emotions. In Union, people fully know that their true nature is to be One with God, and that the Self is eternal.

"There is nothing in this universe apart from God," wrote the Dutch theosophist J. J. Van der Leeuw (1893–1934), "God is present at every point of the universe and can be approached and experienced at every such point...and, though the awareness is no doubt infinitely greater than the universe which is its creation, every part and particle of that universe, from the tiniest atom to the mightiest planet, is essentially, entirely and thoroughly divine."[125]

Western mysticism calls this knowing, "the peace which passeth all understanding." Serenity comes with the acceptance of life as it is given to each of us. Spiritual homecoming is complete.

> We shall not cease from exploration
> And the end of all our exploring
> Will be to arrive where we started
> And know the place for the first time.
>
> —T. S. Eliot [126]

CHAPTER 10

A NEW PSYCHO-SPIRITUAL
WORLDVIEW

All creatures in God and God in all creatures. . .
—Evelyn Underhill (1911)

Last year, a wealthy Chinese businessman in his fifties attended a Breathwork workshop I was facilitating. I'll call him Mr. Chen. He was visiting various Ivy League schools in the U.S. in order to recruit talent for his country. He had been spontaneously invited to join my group by Will, one of my Chinese graduate students and the coordinator of the event. When I heard about the visitor, I shared my concerns about his attending with Will, not only because of the language problem, but also because of the lack of interest in psychotherapy and spirituality in China. I could not understand why Mr. Chen would want to participate.

Will had become deeply interested in Breathwork since meeting me and was exploring his own psycho-spiritual process. He told me that he intuitively felt that this influential man should come because, if he had a positive experience, he might be able to play a part in bringing such a practice to the Chinese people. "Because of communism and atheism, questions of the inner life have been denied for 50 years in my culture, and people are empty inside," Will explained. "They are increasingly searching for something beyond their newly acquired wealth. There is no spiritual support and much discomfort and emotional distress."

So Mr. Chen came, along with a translator. He was distinguished, dressed with tie and jacket, and stood out in the much younger, casually dressed group of grad students. He seemed both attentive and involved. I noticed that during the Breathwork session, he was lying absolutely still and appeared to be in a very deep state of expanded consciousness.

In our sharing circle afterwards Mr. Chen began by saying in broken English that he had just experienced "the best sleep of his life." I questioned him further because he had not looked like he was sleeping. Eventually he was able to call his experience "a dream." So I had to explain then that it was neither sleep nor a dream, but an expanded state of spiritual consciousness. He initially seemed unsettled by my explanation because atheism does not acknowledge such things—it is either a dream or it is nothing.

I then encouraged Mr. Chen to share the pastel drawing he had made of his experience. It was beautifully colored, with many shades blending into one another. In the center, there was a ball of pulsating, brilliant white light. As he tried haltingly to express himself, this very busy assertive Chinese businessman suddenly had tears in his eyes, and simply said thank you, smiling gently and nodding at me. I nodded back, my eyes also filled with tears. In spite of atheism, language and cultural difficulties and a worldview at total odds with his Breathwork experience, Mr. Chen's soul opened and showed him his true spiritual nature. There was also Tracey, an African-American woman. Her Breathwork experience reflected what she called her "spiritual empowerment." An image of herself as a beautiful African goddess in brilliant tribal clothing, dancing with all of the animals of Africa, had arisen in her consciousness. She told us that suddenly Jesus had appeared in the midst of this vision, his arms spread wide, embracing them all. She said that this one experience had brought together for her the power of the feminine, her connection to her cultural origins, and also, with the appearance of Jesus, she felt moved when she understood that He could hold all in His arms and make it one.

And there was Marya. Her parents were Sephardic Jews who had emigrated to the U.S. from Iran when she was a young child. They were living the American dream in California. She was experiencing a lot of conflict between her sense of spiritual longing and the inexorable pull of the typical American lifestyle of a 20-something grad student. A few years earlier, when this conflict first began, she had decided to explore her Middle Eastern roots and had spent time in an orthodox Jewish seminary in Israel. In spite of her confusion about her life's focus, this visit had turned out to be profoundly meaningful.

In the group circle, Marya shared that during the first part of the Breathwork experience she had felt an intense pressure on her chest. "All at once there was a very strong, salty taste in the back of my throat," she said, "and I felt myself drowning in a beautiful, clear, blue-green body of water. I remember wondering if I was drowning in the Dead Sea. I was terrified, but then, everything seemed to stop. After a period of what felt like a deep sleep, I found myself in an incredibly calm and peaceful place. And then, behind closed eyes I saw a large, beautiful hand. I knew immediately that it was the *Chamsa*, the "protective hand of God," as it is called in Israel and the Middle East,

Marya began to weep, saying, "I get it now; I finally get it."

What Marya "got" was the deep awareness that her drowning in the Dead Sea and the symbol of the *Chamsa* were clear messages about her spiritual identity. She, Mr. Chen, and Tracey all experienced contact with the sacred during their Breathwork session. Such examples have become commonplace in Breathwork retreats as people of different cultures and belief systems come to seek a new way of knowing and being.

Mr. Chen came from a culture on the other side of the world. Tracey and Marya had grown up in America, but their religious and cultural roots were a strong influence in their lives, causing in Marya's case confusion about her life path and spiritual identity. And yet, with all of this diversity, it is clear that when peoples' souls open up, the same powerful spiritual energy comes alive, whether we call it God, Buddha, or by the name of an African goddess.

What then is the lesson from these stories? First, to know that when we contact that deep center in the soul, our spiritual roots will always manifest and show us our true identity and a path to becoming whole. It is innate; even if we turn away, the energy does not disappear, but remains there, waiting to be accessed at another time.

It is also important to keep in mind that even though all spiritual traditions—East, West, North and South—will ultimately lead to Oneness, in order to authentically accept others, we must first know and accept all of the influences that make us who we are. With this knowledge, we will finally be able to transcend the dualities and splits that keep us separate from our true nature, from one another, and from God. This is what the global community is longing for, a revitalization of the authentic spiritual journey.

A New Psycho-Spiritual Worldview

As our world community continues to evolve and create unprecedented challenges, help from our support systems is crucial. If a psycho-spiritual worldview were to be absorbed into our culture, both dimensions of reality, the material and the sacred, would be accepted. It would be understood that the Western soul needs healing, that spirituality is a developmental process, and that breakdowns and breakthroughs are all part of the process. Experiences of expanded consciousness—even if confusing—would be trusted and validated. Those individuals who experience spiritual crises—including those with a diagnosis of mental illness—would be supported and guided to trust that the process of going through darkness would eventually bring them into the light.

Some Final Thoughts about Mental Illness in the West

As we come to the end of this book, I want to return to the challenge in our culture concerning what we call "mental illness." Please be clear that I am not in any sense negating the suffering of the millions of people who have been given psychiatric diagnoses and have been told that they have a problem with the brain. Nor am I negating the work of the many dedicated mental health professionals who wish to diminish this suffering; I honor their commitment. My heart aches for the families who witness the pain of loved ones who have such diagnoses.

All the same, we have gotten it wrong. Just because a person with a diagnosis of schizophrenia has a brain that looks different from a "normal brain" should not be considered evidence that the person needs medication to "fix it." Brain research shows that when consciousness expands, it can cause physiological changes in the brain—changes that are very similar to a nun in prayer, a Buddhist monk meditating, or a person who is said to be having a psychotic break.

Neuropsychiatrists Andrew Newberg, and Eugene D'Aquli, authors of *Why God Won't Go Away,* have been studying the relationship between religious experience and brain function with a high-tech imaging camera (SPECT). Their hypothesis suggests that, "spiritual experience, at its very root, is intimately interwoven with human biology. That biology, in some way, compels the spiritual urge."[127] As pointed out in the first chapter, if the physical body knows how to heal itself, why not the non-visible parts that make up a human being? Here is how the authors put it:

> [We] believe that we saw evidence of a neurological process that has evolved to allow us humans to transcend material existence and acknowledge and connect with a deeper, more spiritual part of ourselves, perceived of as an absolute, universal reality that connects us to all that is.[128]

What are the implications? Simply, it tells us to not consider the "religious ideation" of persons as a sure sign of psychopathology and psychosis. Throughout this book, we have read of saints, mystics, ordinary people, and those with a diagnosis of mental illness. In Chapter 6, "Light and Darkness" we read how we are all on a continuum between light and darkness. We all have unresolved shadow material that shows itself as emotional and psychological pain. As I have witnessed in countless cases, the greater the light that comes through consciousness, the more shadow is also pushed to the surface.

What challenges we humans have to face! How wonderfully complex we are—and so fragile at the same time. Isn't it time that we accept the difficulties and the mystery, and open to the possibility that mental illness is not entirely what we think? How would our world be different if we eliminated the labeling? What if we saw a James Holmes, the shooter in the infamous Colorado theater shooting, for example, not as a monster who became "The Joker" because his brain was diseased, but as someone who got drawn into a very dark altered state of consciousness through his obsessions with video games, so much so that he ended up trapped and unable to find his way out—with horrific consequences.

Tragically, there are many more examples of people who somehow are unexpectedly tapping into the deepest parts of their nature, that place where the spiritual converges with the emotional. Above all, what such people need is a wise spiritual teacher to encourage them to choose the light instead of the darkness, to affirm for them that they are children of God.

Again, only by recognizing the spiritual nature of every single person will we be able to recognize our own. Perhaps the suffering and the growing numbers of people like Holmes will be a tragic wake-up call, and not-so-gently push us to realize what we do not yet accept. All of the recent "mentally ill" killers knew they were in serious trouble and asked for help before their shocking acts of violence occurred. All of them were given medication, which did not prevent the tragedies. Those psychotherapists who were monitoring their progress failed them at a terrible cost.

Said the monk and mystic Thomas Merton (1915–1968):

> We stumble and fall constantly, even when we are enlightened. But when we are in true spiritual darkness, we do not even know that we have fallen.[129]

At such times, we need a *Chamsa*, a protective hand that reaches out with strength, love, and hope.

The task before us may seem great, but when the original impulses underlying religion, psychology, and the New Age movement are understood, a healing of the Western Soul will be possible. Western spirituality and religion has at its core the mystical experience, based on the understanding that humans can make a direct connection with God, without the mediation of institutions and external authorities. Psychology was originally based on the understanding that we have a higher self that can guide us.[130] When we learn to access our soul's wisdom, we have everything we need to create peace and happiness. And finally, the original contribution of Transpersonal Psychology and the New Age movement provides numerous ways to make a direct connection with the sacred by expanding consciousness through meditation practices, contemplation, and prayer, as well as Breathwork.

All three visions reflect the deepest principles of Western culture, where the free-thinking individual strives to grow and become more loving, wise, successful, and generous.

As we move ever more into a global society, tremendous tensions in the direction of secularism and diversity are taking us away from our roots. When a culture begins to collapse, as Western culture seems to be doing, belief systems, worldviews, and cultural identity invariably become confused and chaotic.

Yet out of the fear and chaos, revitalizing rituals, dreams, and visions reflecting our Western mystical roots have the opportunity to surface. When the Western Spiritual Path is better understood, the essential message of unconditional love, as exemplified by Jesus' life, can be fully brought into our troubled world. However one thinks of Jesus, it must be acknowledged that his life, teachings, and legacy have had, and still have, an enormous impact on the Western psyche. This means that the rift between Judaism and Christianity cries out for healing. Western culture needs to revisit and renew the relationship with Jesus, the Jewish rabbi, healer, sage, and mystic.

If the existence and purpose of the Soul were widely acknowledged, we would recover awareness of our inner template in which Union is natural and separation is unnatural. With such a worldview, it is possible to understand that life is not about fitting a spiritual reality into the "real world," but the reverse. It is about fitting the mundane into the reality of the spirit.

END NOTES

Introduction: Why the Western Soul Needs Healing

1. Parents for Megan's Law and the Crime Victims Center Survey, 2013.

2. National Institute of Mental Health (NIMH), Washington, DC.

3. NIMH.

4. Pew Forum on Religion and Public Life, 2007.

5. "'Nones' on the Rise," Pew Research Religion & Public Life Project, October 9, 2012 http://www.pewforum.org/2012/10/09/nones-on-the-rise-religion/.

6. Trinity College, Survey on Christianity, Hartford, CT, 2009.

7. The S3K Synagogue Studies Institute report, written by Professors Steven M. Cohen and Lawrence A. Hoffman of Hebrew Union College, 2008.

7a. Young-Eisendrath, P. and Dawson, T. (1997). *The Cambridge Companion to Jung*, Cambridge University Press, p. 319.

Chapter One: Two Ways of Knowing

8. Smith, Huston, *Forgotten Truth: The Primordial Tradition*, NY: Harper Collins, 1976.

9. Schweitzer, Albert, *Reverence for Life: Sermons, 1900–1919*. Harper & Row, 1993, p. 78.

10. Jung, Carl, *Modern Man in Search of a Soul*, New York: Harcourt, Brace and World, 1933.

11. Wilber, Ken, *The Spectrum of Consciousness,* 2nd ed. 1993 Theosophical Publishing House, Wheaton, IL, pp. 33–34.

12. Ibid, pp. 17–36.

12a. Plato, in *Phadaerus,* 370 BC, attributed to Socrates.

13. Cohen, Andrew, *EnlightenNext*, Issue 42, Dec. 2008-February, 2009, p. 42.

Chapter Two: A Crack Between the Worlds

14. http://www.merriam-webster.com/dictionary/epiphenomenon.

14a. C.G. Jung, *The Archetypes of the Collective Unconscious,* 2nd Edition, Routledge, London, 1996, p. 43.

15. Otto, Rudolf, *Mysticism: East and West,* Wheaton, IL: Quest Books, 1987 (First publication in 1932).

16. Jung 1973, 1: 377.

17. Underhill, Evelyn, *Mysticism: A Study in Nature and Development of Spiritual Consciousness,* NY: Doubleday, 1990, p. 72.

18. Ibid, p. 8.

19. Tolle, Eckhart. *The Power of Now: A Guide to Spiritual Enlightenment,* New World Library, 2010, p. 2.

20. Ibid.

21. Ibid.

22. Ibid, p. 3.

23. Assagioli, R. (1989). "Self-Realization and psychological disturbances," in S. Grof and C. Grof (Eds.), *Spiritual Emergency: When Personal Transformation Becomes a Crisis.* Los Angeles, CA: Tarcher, p. 36.

24. Newberg, Andrew, D'Aquili, and Rause, Vince, NY: Ballentine, 2001, p. 9.

25. Grof and Grof, (1989), Self-realization and psychological disturbances, (back cover).

26. Clay, Sally, Center for Multicultural Development, CA Institute for Mental Health, Mental Health and Spirituality Initiative, "Recovery as a Spiritual Journey."

27. Ibid.

28. Ibid.

29. Underhill, E., *Mysticism,* pp. 4–5.

Chapter Three: Worldviews and Support Systems

30. http://www.sylviahartwright.com/coroadc.pdf.

31. Freud, Sigmund, "A Philosophy of Life," Lecture 35, in *New Introductory Lectures on Psychoanalysis,* UK: Hogarth Press, UK, (now imprint of Crown Publishing), NY: Random House, 1932.

32. Ellis, Albert, *Reason and Emotion in Psychotherapy,* NY: Carol, 1991.

33. Burns, David, *The Feeling Good Handbook,* NY: Morrow, 1989.

34. Pavlov, I. *Conditioned Reflexes: An Investigation of the Physiological Activity of the Cerebral Cortex.* Translated and edited by GV Anrep, London: Oxford University Press, 1927.

35. Seligman, Martin, *Authentic Happiness: Using the New Positive Psychology to Realize Your Potential for Lasting Fulfillment,* NY: Free Press, 2002.

36. Maslow, Abraham, *Toward a Psychology of Being,* Wiley, 3rd Edition, 1998.

37. http://en.wikipedia.org/wiki/Gestalt_prayer.

38. http://www.authentichappiness.sas.upenn.edu/Default.aspx.

39. From 1990 to the end of 1999, the Library of Congress and the National Institute of Mental Health (NIMH) sponsored a unique interagency initiative "to enhance public awareness of the benefits to be derived from brain research." More information can be found on nimhinfo@nih.gov.

40. Doctors at the University of Maryland School of Medicine are testing a "pacemaker for the brain," that may turn out to be a treatment for depression. They think it may work for patients who have not responded to psychotherapy or drugs. The device is a battery-powered electrical pulse generator, implanted under the skin on the upper left side of a patient's chest. It sends intermittent low-level pulses of electricity to the vagus nerve in the neck. Those pulses, said

Mitchell a. King, M.D., appears to stimulate an area of the brain that regulates mood. *International News,* July 6, 2009.

41. Jackson, Grace MD, *Rethinking Psychiatric Drugs,* Authorhouse, 2005; Valenstein, Elliot, *Blaming the Brain: The Truth About Drugs and Mental Health,* Free Press, 2002; Scott, Timothy, *America Fooled: The Truth About Antidepressants, Antipsychotics and How We've Been Deceived,* 2006; Breggin, Peter, *Medication Madness,* St. Martins Press, 2008; Whitfield, Charles MD, *The Truth About Mental Illness,* Health Communications, 2004; *The Truth About Depression,* Health Communications, 2003, and many others.

42. Lajoie, D.H. and Shapiro, "SI, Definitions of Transpersonal Psychology: The First 23 Years," *Journal of Transpersonal Psychology,* Vol. 24, 1992.

43. Turner, R.P., Lukoff, D., Barnhouse, R.T., Lu, F.G., *Journal of Nervous and Mental Disease,* 1995, July; 183(7): 435-44. Department of Psychiatry, University of California, San Francisco.

44. http://spiritualemergency.blogspot.com/2006/01/personal-account-dr-david-lukoff.html.

Chapter Four: God Experience

45. http://www.gallup.com/poll/147887/Americans-Continue-Believe-God.aspx.

46. Lewis, David (translator), 1904, *The Life of St. Teresa of Jesus, of the Order of Our Lady of Carmel* (c.1565), at Project Gutenberg, Ch. XXIX, pp.16-17.

47. Anonymous, Late 14th century, *The Cloud of Unknowing,* NY: Harper Collins, 2010.

48. Seigel, Ronald, *Fire in the Brain: Clinical Tales of Hallucination,* NY: Plume, 1993.

49. Vedantam, Shankar, "Tracing the Synapses of our Spirituality," *Washington Post,* July 17, 2001.

50. Luhrmann, T.H., *When God Talks Back: Understanding the American Evangelical Relationship with God,* NY: Vintage, 2012.

51. Anonymous, Late 14th century, *The Cloud of Unknowing*, NY: Harper Collins, 2010.

52. Wilber, Ken, *Integral Spirituality: A Startling New Role for Religion in the Modern and Postmodern World*, Shambhala, 2007.

53. Goodall, Jane and Berman, Phillip, *Reason for Hope: A Spiritual Journey*, Grand Central Publishing (3rd. ed.), 2000, p. 173.

54. http://www.context.org/iclib/ic34/spangler/.

55. Jung, Carl, *The Psychology of the Transference*, Routledge, 1983, p. 82.

56. Wilber, Ken, *What is Enlightenment*, Issue 33, 2006, p. 87.

57. Ibid, p. 87.

58. Rinpoche, Sogyal and Gaffney, Patrick, *The Tibetan Book of Living and Dying*, San Francisco: Harper, 2012, p. 289.

59. Ibid, p. 288.

60. Ibid, p. 288.

61. Jung, Carl, *Memories, Dreams, and Reflections*, NY: Vintage Books, 1989, p. 88.

Chapter Five: Mystical Ground

62. Smith, Paul, R., *Integral Christianity: The Spirit's Call to Evolve*, Paragon House, St. Paul, Minnesota, 2011.

63. Burnshaw Stanley (ed.), Carmi, T., Glassman, Susan and Hirschfield, Ariel, *The Modern Hebrew Poem Itself*, Wayne State University Press, 2002, p. 43.

64. Erikson, Erik, *Identity and the Life Cycle*, NY, Norton, 1980.

65. Toynbee, Arnold J. and Urban, GR, *Toynbee on Toynbee: A Conversation Between Arnold Toynbee and GR Urban*, NY: Oxford University Press, 1974; Hevda, Ben Israel, "Debate With Toynbee, Herzog, Talmon, Friedman," *Israel Studies*, Spring 2006, Vol. 11, Issue 1, pp 79-90; "Counseling and Values," Oct. 1, 2004, *Relationship of Ethnic Identity and Spiritual Development*; Bergin, A.E., *Values and Religious Issues in Psychotherapy and Mental Health*, American

Psychologist, 46, 394-403; Smith, Timothy, "The Spiritual Self: Toward a Conceptualization of Spiritual Identity Development," *Journal of Psychology and Theology,* June 22, 2003; Fowler, J. *Stages of Faith: The Psychology of Human Development and the Quest for Meaning,* San Francisco: Harper and Row, 1981.

66.   Moore, Thomas, *Care of the Soul,* NY: Harper Collins, 1992, p. 121.

67.   Dali Lama.

68.   Buber, Martin, *The Legend of Baal-Shem,* NY: Random House, 1987.

69.   Buber, Martin, *I and Thou,* Scribner, NY, 1958, p.101.

70.   Matthew 3:16–17.

71.   Abelson, J., M.D., D.Lit., *Jewish Mysticism,* London: G. Bell and Sons, 1913, p. 17.

72.   Miller, Ron and Bernstein, Laura, *Healing the Jewish Christian Rift,* Woodstock, VT: Skylight Paths, 2006.

73.   Matthew 4:17.

74.   *Gnosis,* "Kabbalah: Exploring the Roots of Mysticism," Vol. 3, 1986-87; Hoffman, Edward, *The Way of Splendor,* Boston: Shambhala, 1981; Lancaster, Brian L., *The Essence of Kabbalah,* Arctures, London, 2006; Frankel, Estelle, *Sacred Therapy,* Boston: Shambhala, 2005; Epstein, Perle, Kabbalah, Boston: Shambhala, 2001.

75.   Ladinsky, Daniel. *Love Poems from God: Twelve Sacred Voices from the East and West,* Penguin Group, 2002, p. 129.

Chapter Six: Light and Darkness

76.   Hitler, Adolf, *Mein Kampf,* Germany: Eher Verlag, 1925.

77.   Hitler, Adolf in Sklar, D., *The Nazis and the Occult,* NY: Dorset Press, p. 104.

78.   PBS video (Frontline production), "Faith and Doubt at Ground Zero," 2002.

79.   Toynbee, Arnold, *Study of History,* Volumes 1 and 2, Oxford

University Press, UK, 1987.

80. St. Teresa of Avila, *The Life of Teresa of Jesus*, NY: Doubleday, 1991.

81. http://www.cnn.com/2013/09/25/us/washington-navy-yard-investigation/index.html?hpt=hp_t3.

82. Weil, Simone and Wills, Arthur, *Gravity and Grace*, p. 24.

Chapter Seven: The First Stage: Spiritual Awakening

84. Nietzche, Friederich, *The Portable Nietzsche*, Penguin Books, 1977, p. 307.

85. Erikson, Erik, *Identity and the Life Cycle*, NY: WW Norton, 1994.

86. http://www.nytimes.com/2011/10/30/opinion/mona-simpsons-eulogy-for-steve-jobs.html?pagewanted=all&_r=0.

87. Underhill, Evelyn, *Mysticism: A Study in the Nature and Development of Spiritual Consciousness*, (1911), 12th edition, NY: Doubleday, 1990.

88. Progoff, Ira in Underhill, *Mysticism*, p. vii, 1990.

89. Campbell, Joseph, *Hero With a Thousand Faces*, 2nd edition, NJ: Princeton University Press, 1972.

90. James, William, *The Varieties of Religious Experience*, General Books LLC, 2012, (First Publication, 1902).

91. Eliade, Mircea, *The Sacred and the Profane*, San Diego, CA: Harcourt Brace Jovanovich, 1987 (First Publication, 1959).

92. Ibid. Eliade, (all quotes from pp. 10-14).

93. Ibid. Eliade.

94. Hoffman, Edward, *The Way of Splendor*, Shambhala, Boston, 1981, p. 152.

95. P.D. Ouspensky.

95a. http://www.theosophytrust.org/285-isaac-luria

Chapter Eight: The Second Stage: Illumination

96. Viviano, Benedict, *The Kingdom of God in History,* Wilmington, DE: Michael Glazier, 1988; Dehaven-Smith, *The Hidden Teachings of Jesus: The Political Meaning of the Kingdom of God,* MI: Phanes Press, 1994: Borg, Marcus, *Jesus, A New Vision,* San Francisco: Harper, 1987.

97. Hopkins, Gerard Manley, *God's Grandeur: Poems and Prose,* Penguin Classics, 1985, p. 27.

98. Underhill, Evelyn, Ruysbroeck, London: G. Bell, 1915, p. 2.: "De vera Contemplations", cap. xi.

99. Blake, William, *The Letters of William Blake,* Edited by A.G.B. Russell, London, 1906, p. 171.

100. Hilton, Walter in Underhill, Evelyn, *Mysticism,* 1990, p. 264.

101. Kook, Rav Abraham Isaac, *A Thirst For the Living God,* translated by Jacobson, Burt in *Gnosis, Kabbalah,* No. 3, 1986-87, p.13.

102. Hildegard of Bingen in Underhill, Evelyn, *Mysticism,* 1990, p. 249.

103. Kook, Rav Abraham Isaac, "A Thirst For a Living God," in *Gnosis,* No. 3, 1986-7, p. 15.

104. Reverend Jim Jones, (1931-1978), founder and leader of "Peoples Temple," which is best known for the Nov. 18, 1978 mass suicide of 913 Temple members in Jonestown, Guyana; Sai Baba, (1926-2011) was an Indian Guru, spiritual figure, mystic, and educator revered by millions of devotees.

105. "Dark Night of the Soul" has been referenced by St. John of the Cross, Madame Guyon, Lucie Christine, Suso, Meister Eckhart, St. Gertrude, Ruysbroeck, and St. Catherine of Siena in Underhill, *Mysticism,* pp. 380-412.

106. May, Gerald, *The Dark Night of the Soul,* Harper San Francisco, 2004; Moore, Thomas, *Dark Nights of the Soul,* Penguin, NY, 2005.

107. De Caussade in Underhill, Evelyn, *Mysticism,* p. 390.

108. Saint John of the Cross in Underhill, *Mysticism,* p. 399.

109. Psalms 22: 1, Matthew 27:46, Mark 15:34.

110. Moore, Thomas, *Dark Nights of the Soul*, Penguin, NY, 2005.

Chapter Nine: The Third Stage: Union

111. Black Elk. *Black Elk Speaks: Being the Life Story of a Holy Man of the Ogala Sioux as told to John G. Neihardt (Flaming Rainbow)*, NY: Morrow, 1932. Reprint, Lincoln: Univ. of Nebraska Press, 1979.

112. *Qur'an*. Translations of the Qur'an, Surah 57: Al-Hadid.

113. R. Maitri *Upanishad*, 6.17.

114. Rabbi Nathan of Nemerov, Likutey Moharan 11, 56 in Frankel, p. 68.

115. See Eliezer Shore, "Solomon's request" *Parabola*, Fall, 2002, pp. 56-59.

116. "Maggid of Mezritch" in Matt, Daniel, *The Essential Kabbalah*, Harper One, NY, 1996, p. 71.

117. *John of the Cross: Selected Writings*, Kavanaugh, Kieran, OCD (trans.), Paulist Press, 1988, p. 78.

118. Frankel, Estelle, *Sacred Therapy*, Boston: Shambhala, 2005, p. 75.

119. Hymn 27, pp.125-132.

120. Suri, Ankur and Suri, R.P., *Inspiring Quotes of Socrates, Plato, and Aristotle*, Kindle Edition, 2011.

121. St Paul in Galatians 2:20, as quoted by Underhill, Evelyn, *Mysticism*, p. 417.

122. Carey, Ken, *Starseed Transmissions*, San Francisco: Harper, 1991, p. 15.

123. Fox, Matthew, *The Coming of the Cosmic Christ*, San Francisco: Harper, 1988, p. 1.

124. Harvey Andrew, *Son of Man: The Mystical Path to Christ*, NY: Tarcher/Putnam, 1998, p. 117.

125. Van der Leeuw, 1893. *The Fire of Creation*. Reprint of the edition published in the Theosophical Press, 1976, pp. 7-8.

126. Eliot, T.S., Little Gidding, in *The Four Quartets,* Mariner Books, 1968, p. 47.

Chapter 10: A New Psycho-Spiritual Worldview

127. Newberg, A., D'Aquili, E., *Why God Won't Go Away,* NY: Ballantine, 2001.

128. Ibid. p.9.

129. Merton, T., *Thoughts in Solitude,* NY: Macmillan, 2011, p. 38.

130. Gustav, F., *On Life After Death,* (1882), Maryland: Wildside Press, 2012.

INDEX

A

Abelson, Joshua, 105

Adams, Douglas, 17

Agnosticism, 72

Alexis, Aaron, 127–128

Alienation, 155–158

Analytical Psychology (Jung school), 23–24

Angels, 123
brown angels, 49
presence, 7–8

Anger, replacement, 72–73

Anti-psychotic medication, usage, 121–122

Approach-avoidance tendency, 185

"Asking Big Questions," 150–151

Assagioli, Robert, 35–36

Auschwitz (concentration camp), pilgrimage, 132

Awakening, 144
challenges, resolution, 159–160
shadow, 170

Ayin, 191–192

B

Beck, Aaron, 52–53

Behaviorism, 52–53

Being, experience, 190

Belief system, worldviews, 44–45

Bipolar disorder, xviii, 121–122

Black Elk, Chief, 190

Blake, William, 172–173

Blessing, 86–87

Blinding light, experience, 7–8

Brain
chemical disruption, 58
condition, examination, 56–60
"Decade of the Brain" (NIMH), 55–56
improvement, 55–56
research, 210

Breathwork, 27, 84, 154, 160, 213
experience, 96–97, 207–208
initiation, 162
method, simplicity, xvii
practice, 200
training sessions, 85
visions, 165–166
workshops, 112, 185, 205

Buddhism, xix

C

Calling, sense, 103

Campbell, Joseph, 41, 145

Cancer, dying (impact), 156

Carey, Ken, 198–199

Chamsa, 208, 212

Choice
commitment, 119–121
importance, 103

Christ consciousness, 198–199
permeation, 201–202
relationships, 202–204

Clay, Sally, 37–38, 59

Cloud of Unknowing, The, 74–75

Co-dependent relationship, impact, 183–184

Cognitive behavioral therapy (CBT), 52–53

Coincidence, consciousness label, 20

Collective mentality, 103–104

Commitment, absence (living problem), 126–127

Compassion
anger replacement, 72–73
relationships, 202–204

Consciousness
confusion, 161–162
control, absence, 22
ecstatic state, 32–33
expansion, xvii, 141, 147, 160, 209
labels, 20–21
level, xxiii–xxiv
access, xvii–xviii
increase, 195
merger, 201
states
differences, 37
heightening, 81
therapy, 26–28
voices, mystical aspect, 125

Creativity, struggle, 131–136

Crown chakra, impact, 3

Culture, lazy assumption, 39

D

Dali Lama, 41, 102

D'Aquli, Eugene, 210

Darkness

creativity, struggle, 131–136
increase, 170–173
light, split, 128
strength, 129–131

Dark night. *See* Soul

Death
fear, 159
mystic death, 180

"Decade of the Brain" (NIMH), 55–56

DeCaussade, Jean Pierre, 180

Deification, 197

Delusions
consciousness label, 20
impact, 157–158

Departure (God journey stage), 145

Depression, xviii
feelings, 177

Depth psychology, 59–60

Diagnostic and Statistical Manual of Mental Disorders (DSM-IV), religious/spiritual problem category, 60

Direct God energy, 81–82

Divine love, experience, 71–75

Divine Presence, sense, 173–174

Do-it-yourself spirituality, problems, 5–7

Dreams, 87, 140
analysis, 160
discussion, 153, 167–168
interpretation, 95
recurrence, 93–94, 99
remembrance, 148–149
revitalization, 213–214

usage, 147–149
Dualism. *See* Western dualism

E

Eastern religions, dominance, 98
Eastern spiritual traditions, lessons, 104
Eating disorders, xviii
Eckhart, Meister, 9, 199
Ego (small self), 9–11
  death, 144, 158
  human-made/finite characteristic, 11
  loss, 158, 180
  dissonance, 159–160
Eliade, Mircea, 147
Eliot, T.S., 204
Ellis, Albert, 52–53
Emotional pain, chemical disruption, 58
Emotional strait jackets, 121–122
Energy, manifestation, 118
Epiphenomena, 21–24
Erikson, Erik, 101–102, 142–143
Evil, reality, 115–116

F

Faith and Doubt at Ground Zero (video), 115
Forgiveness
  anger replacement, 72–73
  relationships, 202–204
Fourth school, 54
Frankel, Estelle (meditation), 191–192

Free association, role, 52
Freud, Sigmund, 51–52, 59
Fulfillment, absence, 163

G

Gestalt prayer, 54
God, 104–106
  alignment, 83–86
  American belief, xix, 69–70
  challenge, 86–87
  choice/commitment, 119–121
  connection, 168, 169
  consciousness, power (recognition), 173
  death, 115
  direct God energy, 81–82
  divine love, experience, 71–75
  dwelling place, 104
  energy, 84
  expression, 9–11
  flow, 77, 119
  experiences, 141
  force, 11
  Immanent, 77
  journey, 145
  living, 191–192
  love, 108–109
  Oneness, 78–80
  partnership, 119–121
  personal experience, 103
  personal relationship, 80–81, 197
  presence, 203–204
  reign, approach, 106–107
  Self, 75–78, 80
  connection, feeling, 77–78
  interplay, 34
  subject, discussion, 70–71
  surrender, 130
  Thou, 80–81

three faces, 75–86
God as All, 83
God-as-All, 79
God-as-Gaia, 79
God as I, 75–78
God as I AM, 83
God as Other, 80–82
God-as-Other, 83
God as the All, 78–80
God-centered reality, 170
Going crazy, fear, 55, 154–155
Goodall, Jane, 78–79
Good/evil, duality, 107–108
Grandiosity, 175–178
Grof, Christina, 37
Grof, Stanislav, xvi–xvii, 25–26, 37
Gyato, Tenzin, 102

H
Hallucination, consciousness label,
    20
Harvey, Andrew, 202–203
Healing experience, 7–9
"Hero's Journey" (Campbell), 145
Hierphany, 147
Higher Power, xix, 177
    belief, absence, 52
    references, shift, 70
Higher self (soul), 9–11
    understanding, 213
Hildegard of Bingen, visions,
    173–174
Hilton, Walter, 173

Hinduism, xix, 9
Hitler, Adolf, 112–113
    legacy, transformation, 131–134
Holmes, James, 211
Holocaust, victims, 134
Holotropic Breathwork, xvi–xvii,
    26
Holy Spirit, energy, 63–64
Hopkins, Gerard Manley, 169–170
Horizon House, counselor role, 18
Human consciousness, 44
Humanistic psychology, 53–54
Humanity/God, love (impact), 202

I
Identity, losing (fear), 185–186
Illumination, 144, 145, 168, 184
    Jewish/Christian perspectives,
        173–174
    spiritual illumination, characteris-
        tics, 169–173
Imagination/fantasy, consciousness
    label, 20
Initiation (God journey stage), 145
Inner darkness, 124
    prevalence, 117–118
Inner life, approach, 18
Inner light, 176–177
    connection, 171
    nonacceptance, 121–124
Inner shadow, 176–177
Inner states, feeling, 32–33
Inner teacher, shift, 172–173
Inner truth, 179

Integral Christianity (Smith), 90

Intention, power, 118–119

International Association of Near-Death Studies (IANDS), 25

Intimacy, fear, 184–185

Isolation, increase, 66

J

James, William, 3, 10, 146

Jesus
  experiences, 101
  identification, 106–107
  mystical experiences, 94–95
  personal union, challenge, 200–202
  transformative power, 91–92
  visions, 97

Jewish Mysticism (Abelson), 105–106

Jobs, Steve, 143

John of Ruysbroeck, 170

John the Baptist, 105, 106

Jung, Carl, 9, 15, 64, 80
  Analytical Psychology, 23–24
  dream, 87
  Freud, relationship, 59
  God energy, 84
  wisdom, 89

K

Kabbalah, 106–108

Knockout (sport), 114–115

Kook, Abraham Isaac, 173–174, 189

Kotzk (rabbi), 104

Krishnamurti, 10

Kundalini awakening, 63–64

L

Life
  meaning, 152
  natural flow, 158
  situation, resolution, 76
  stages, 142–143

Life/soul, tension (increase), 22–23

Light, 124
  belief, 164
  darkness, split, 128
  energy, clarity/alignment, 130
  increase, 170–173
  out-of-body experiences, 100–101
  partnering, 121

Loss, sense, 163

Love, power (relationships), 202–204

Lukoff, Dvid, 61

Luminosity-Emptiness (Union), 190

Luria, Isaac, 155–156

M

Maggid of Mezritch, 191

Maslow, Abraham, 53–54, 167

Matrix Research Institute, 24–25, 27, 84

Mauthausen (concentration camp), 133

May, Rollo, 53–54

Meditation, 160
  sharing, 201

Meditative practice, 5–6
Mein Kampf (Hitler), 113
Mental illness, 139–140
    mental neglect, contrast, 127–129
    reality, 24
Merton, Thomas, 212
Modern worldviews, 45–46
    shift, 48
Moore, Thomas, 102, 179–181
Moyer, Bill, 41
Multidimensional reality, 149–150
Mundaka Upanishad, 190
Mystical experiences, 168
    characteristics, 169–173
Mystic death, 180
Mysticism (Underhill), 27, 144
Mysticism, wellspring, 28–29
"Mystic Way, The," 28, 143–144

N

National Institute of Mental Health
    (NIMH), xviii–xix, 24–25, 55
Nazi
    children/grandchildren, help, 114
    heritage, 112–113
    youth, experience, 114–115
Nazism
    spiritual movement, 133
    unconscious identification, access,
    120
Near-death experience (NDE),
    146, 163
    impact, 165
New Age movement, 59–60
    characteristic, 62–66

standards, 62–63
Newberg, Andrew, 210
Nietzsche, Friedrich, 142–143
Nothingness, 191
Numinous, path, 24

O

Oglala Sioux Nation, 190
Oneness, 78–80, 184, 190
out-of-body experiences, 100
Ouspensky, P.D., 150
Out-of-body experience, 3–4,
    100–101
Overwhelmed, feeling, 178–179

P

Pain
    blunting, medication (usage), 48
    chemical disruption, 58
    issues, 131
    nonresolution, 8
Paranoia, 4
Passion, impact, 29
Passive purification, 180
Pauli, Wolfgang, 84
Peace/bliss, state, 31
Perls, Fritz, 54
Personality problems, xviii
Personal spirituality, conflict, 89
Portland Coalition for the
    Psychiatrically Labeled, 38
Positive psychology, 53
Postmodern worldviews, 45–46
    usage, 47

Power of Now, The (Tolle), 30
Premodern worldviews, 45–46
psychoanalysis, relationship, 52
Premonitions, writing, xxi
Presenting problem, 161
Present moment, power, 31–32
Privation, 180
Process, support, 13–15
Progoff, Ira, 144
Psychoanalysis, 51–52
Pre-modern view, relationship, 52
Psychological development, 8–9
Psychological disturbances, 36
Psychological ego, 59–60
Psychological pain, chemical disruption, 58
Psychology
    depth psychology, 59–60
    Eastern religions, dominance, 98
    humanistic psychology, 53–54
    positive psychology, 53
    spirituality
        avoidance, 54–56
        debate, 124–125
        requirement, 24–26
        support system, theories/worldviews, 51–54
Psychopathology, 211
Psychosis, 211
    consciousness label, 20
    diagnosis, 19–20, 42
Psycho-spiritual work, xvi–xvii, 172, 177
    goals, 13–14
    types, examples, 160–166

Psycho-spiritual worldview, 205, 209
Psychosynthesis, 36
Psychotherapy, 93
    experiences, 164–165
    purpose, 12
    quitting, 25–26
    rational psychotherapy, 52–53
    success, absence, 126–127
Psychotic breakdown, 4
Purgation, 143
Purification, 35
    passive purification, 180

R

Rational psychotherapy, 52–53
Reality
    interpretation, shift, 35
    multidimensional reality, 149–150
Really real (glimpse), dreams (usage), 147–149
Reason for Hope (Goodall), 78
Religion
    offspring, 28
    rejection, xxiii
    support system, 48–51
Religious ideation, 18–19, 211
    consciousness label, 20
Religious past, shame, 96–97
Religious problem, identification, 61
Religious/spiritual problem
    diagnostic category, 60–61
    DSM-IV inclusion, 60
Return (God journey stage), 145

Revelations, depression, 65
Rinpoche, Sogyal, 82
Rituals, revitalization, 213–214
Rogers, Carl, 53–54
Rutman, Irv, 84–86

S

Sacred force, 11
Sacred marriage
    rejection, 92–96
    story, example, 99
Sagan, Carl, 69
Sai Baba (guru), 175–176
Sainthood, 193–194
Scaffolding, 105–106
Schizo-affective disorder, 121–122
Schizophrenia, diagnosis, 210
Schweitzer, Albert, 7
Scientific worldview, 184
Sefer Ketzirah, 106
Self
    awakening, 143
    knowledge, 146
    purification, 116–117
    source, 96
Selfhood, examination, 6
Self-knowledge, 173
    desire, 62–63
Self-realization, 36
self, Self (contrast), 141–142
Seligman, Martin, 53
Shadow, 170
    approach, 35
    avoidance, 64–66

casting, 114
Shadow self, 5
Sharing circle, interactions, 206
Shema (prayer), 105
Sixth sense, 118
Small self (ego), 9–110
Smith, Paul R., 90
Son of Man (Harvey), 202–203
Soul (higher self), 9–11
    abandonment, 181
    contacting, xvi–xviii
    dark night, 144, 179–182, 193
    experiences/knowledge, 10
    healing, 173
Soul-knowledge intuition/insight,
    11
Source, connection, 77
Spangler, David, 79
Spectrum of Consciousness, The
    (Wilber), 9–10
Spiritual autobiography, writing,
    xxi
Spiritual awakening, 145
    challenges, 154–159
    stage, entry, 157–158
Spiritual but not religious (SBNR),
    xix
Spiritual contraindication,
    xviii–xix
Spiritual crisis, 35–38
Spiritual development, xv–xvi,
    8–9, 117
    paradox, 120
    path, 27

Spiritual emergency, 37
Spiritual experiences, 111–112
    attention, 11–12
    chemical disruption, 58
    details, meaning, 20–21
    occurrences, 23–24
    oxytocin, relationship, 74
Spiritual guidance, hunger,
    xx–xxiii
Spiritual healing, 176
Spiritual identity, 101–102
    rejection, 179
Spiritual illumination, 186
    challenges, 174–186
    characteristics, 169–173
    process, 172
    resolution/integration, 186
Spirituality
    absence, 54–56
    interest, 58–59
    psychology, debate, 124–125
    reality, question, 43
    requirement, 24–26
Spiritual journey, stages, 142–143
Spiritual life, absence, 82–83
Spiritual nature, recognition, 212
Spiritual problem, identification,
    61
Spiritual process, control/edit,
    182–183
Spiritual search, xxiii–xxiv
Spiritual traditions, universal/
    cross-cultural commonalities,
    63
Spiritual transcendence, state, 33

Stage, sustaining, 33
Starseed Transmissions, The
    (Carey), 198–199
St. Augustine, 3
St. John of the Cross, 180, 191
St. Symeon the New Theologian,
    194
St. Teresa of Avila, 126
St. Thomas Aquinas, 108–109
    Gnostic Gospel, 189
Study of History (Toynbee), 117
Sufism, xix
Suicide, xviii
    attempt, 163
Support systems
    psychology, 51–54
    religion, relationship, 48–50
    trust, 49–50
    worldview basis, 45–46
Synchronicity, 84–86, 178–179

T

Tchernichovsky, Shaul, 99
Teresa of Avila, 73
Third eye, impact, 3
*Tibetan Book of Living and Dying,
    The* (Rinpoche), 82
Tikkun (usage), 198
Tikkun Olam, 198
Tillich, Paul, 139
Tolle, Eckhart (mystical experi-
    ence), 29–32
Toward a Psychology of Being
    (Maslow), 53–54

Toynbee, Arnold, 117
Transcendent, glimpse, 154–155
    first characteristic, 146–147
    second characteristic, 150–151
Transference, role, 52
Transpersonal psychology, 59–60
Treatment, provision, 13–15
Trust, mistrust (contrast), 142–143
Turba Philosophorum, 69

U

Underhill, Evelyn, 27–29, 39,
    90–91, 143–144, 205
Union, 144, 145, 184
    centering, 197
    experience, 191–192, 195
    methods, 196–199
    final stage, 183, 189–190
    longing, 183–186
    Luminosity-Emptiness, 190
    premature state, 32–35, 193
    problem, psychology perspective,
        193–196
Upanishads, 89

V

Van der Leeuw, J.J., 203–204
Virgin Mary, appearance, 19
Visions, 165–166, 178–179
    revitalization, 213–214
    writing, xxi
Voices, 178–179
    identification, 124–126

W

Western dualism, 116–117
Western mystical roots, influence
    (discounting), 63–64
Western path
    activity, 102–104
    form, 198–199
Western seekers, 98–99
Western spiritual DNA, 90–91
Western spiritual imagery, recog-
    nition, 99
Western Spiritual Path, 34, 141
    developmental stages, 145
    model, revision, 145
    stages, 143–146
    thoughts, 187–188
Why God Won't Go Away
    (Newberg/D'Aquli), 210
Wilber, Ken, 9, 10, 80
Worldviews, 44–45, 51–54
    basis, 45–46
    demand, 47–48
    scientific worldview, 184
    types, 45
Worldwide communication, desire,
    62–63

Z

Zalman (rabbi) ("The Gaon"), 147
Zusya (rabbi), 102